THE
SUNNY SIDE
OF
THE ALPS

HENRY HOLT
AND COMPANY
New York

THE SUNNY SIDE OF THE ALPS

YEAR-ROUND DELIGHTS IN
SOUTH TYROL AND
THE DOLOMITES

PAUL HOFMANN

Henry Holt and Company, Inc.
Publishers since 1866
115 West 18th Street
New York, New York 10011

Henry Holt ® is a registered
trademark of Henry Holt and Company, Inc.

Published in Canada by Fitzhenry & Whiteside Ltd.,
195 Allstate Parkway, Markham, Ontario L3R 4T8.

Library of Congress Cataloging-in-Publication Data
Hofmann, Paul.
The sunny side of the Alps: year-round delights in South Tyrol
and the Dolomites/Paul Hofmann.—1st ed.
            p.   cm.
Includes bibliographical references and index.
1. Trentino-Alto Adige (Italy)—Description and travel.
2. Trentino-Alto Adige (Italy)—Guidebooks.   3. Dolomite Alps
(Italy)—Description and travel.   4. Dolomite Alps
(Italy)—Guidebooks.   I. Title.
DG975.T792H6   1995   94-3844
914.5'38304929—dc20   CIP

ISBN 0-8050-3259-2
ISBN 0-8050-4710-7 (An Owl Book: pbk.)

Henry Holt books are available for special promotions
and premiums. For details contact: Director, Special Markets.

First published in hardcover in 1995 by
Henry Holt and Company, Inc.

First Owl Book Edition—1996

Book design by Claire Vaccaro
Map design by Jackie Aher

Printed in the United States of America
All first editions are printed on acid-free paper.∞

1   3   5   7   9   10   8   6   4   2
1   3   5   7   9   10   8   6   4   2
(pbk.)

CONTENTS

CONTENTS

CONTENTS

Accommodations · Languages · Best Time to Visit;
Weather · Food and Drink · Shopping;
Business Hours · Information

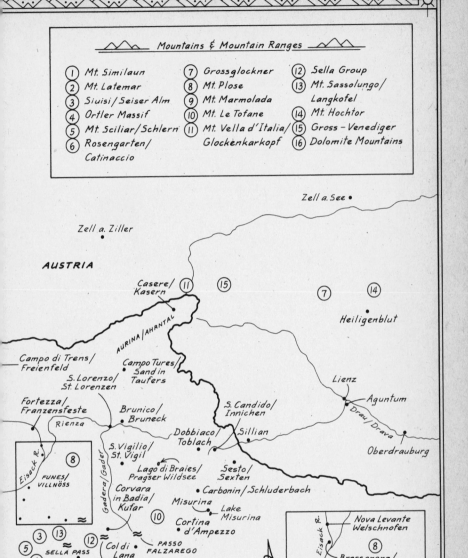

Mountains & Mountain Ranges

1. Mt. Similaun
2. Mt. Latemar
3. Siuisi / Seiser Alm
4. Ortler Massif
5. Mt. Sciliar / Schlern
6. Rosengarten / Catinaccio
7. Grossglockner
8. Mt. Plose
9. Mt. Marmolada
10. Mt. Le Tofane
11. Mt. Vella d'Italia / Glockenkarkopf
12. Sella Group
13. Mt. Sassolungo / Langkofel
14. Mt. Hochtor
15. Gross – Venediger
16. Dolomite Mountains

Zell a. See

Zell a. Ziller

AUSTRIA

Casere / Kasern

Heiligenblut

AURINA / AHRNTAL

Campo di Trens / Freienfeld

Campo Tures / Sand in Taufers

S. Lorenzo / St. Lorenzen

Lienz

Aguntum

Fortezza / Franzensfeste

Brunico / Bruneck

S. Candido / Innichen

Drau / Drava

Rienza

Dobbiaco / Toblach

Sillian

Oberdrauburg

Eisack R.

FUNES / VILLNÖSS

S. Vigilio / St. Vigil

Lago di Braies / Pragser Wildsee

Sesto / Sexten

Gadera / Gader

Corvara in Badia / Kutar

Carbonin / Schluderbach

Misurina

Lake Misurina

Cortina d'Ampezzo

Nova Levante Welschnofen

Eisack R.

Sella Pass

Col di Lana

PASSO FALZAREGO

North

Chiusa / Klausen

Bressanone / Brixen

Canazei

CAMPOLONGO PASS

Pieve di Cadore

FUNES / VILLÖSS

Laion / Lajen

Lago di Carezza / Karersee

Canale d'Agordo

Castelrotto / Kastelruth

PASSO GARDENA / GRÖDNER JOCH

Moena

Ortisei / Urtijëi

ITALY

Agordo

S. Christina

I.

FRIENDLY
MOUNTAINS

જીક

The Alpine arc that sweeps from the Swiss Engadine to the Slovenian forests has been inhabited since the Stone Age, as is evidenced by the mummified body of a hunter or shepherd discovered in a glacier nearly 10,000 feet (3,200 meters) above sea level close to the Italian-Austrian border in 1991. Scientists determined that the man lived and died 5,300 years ago.

The Brenner and the other Alpine passes saw traders and adventurers long before the legions of Emperor Augustus marched up to and beyond them. German kings and emperors crossed the Brenner Pass more than sixty times in the Middle Ages and during the Renaissance era on their way to being crowned by the pope, to embarking on a Crusade, or to intervening in Italian or Mediterranean power struggles.

During the last two centuries countless other travelers and guests have sought the sun and repose, cures from various ills, or the challenges of the Dolomite peaks and other mountains in the Alpine heartland. They have consistently been welcomed by its friendly inhabitants.

Franz Kafka, already ailing, went to Merano to breathe easier in its famously mild air. He was overwhelmed. He wrote to an acquaintance, Milena Jesenská, that he had found the most beautiful landscape he had ever seen. An epistolary affair started, which was to result in his celebrated *Letters to Milena*.

Sigmund Freud's womenfolk loved Merano. His wife stayed there several times, and he visited the town with his sister-in-law Minna Bernays during a lengthy trip south of the main crest of the Alps. Anna, Freud's favorite child, perused his books at the age of seventeen when she stayed five months in the Tyrolean resort to recuperate from surgery and from the stress of high school graduation exams in Vienna, which she had passed with distinction.

Decades later Ezra Pound found refuge near Merano after his release from United States custody. The poet, a wartime supporter of Italian fascism, busied himself in the garden of the dilapidated castle in which his daughter and son-in-law had made their home and often took his grandchildren to town for gelato. Pound had maples and vines planted and tried to talk local vintners into growing soybeans instead of wine; fortunately they didn't heed him.

In another South Tyrolean village below an age-old Alpine gateway, the Brenner Pass, the white-haired Henrik Ibsen was writing his tenderly bitter *Wild Duck* when he fell in love with a Viennese girl forty-three years his junior. He spoke to her of divorcing his wife to be free to marry her. Nothing, however, came of his infatuation.

A few years later Gustav Mahler started spending summers in yet another part of South Tyrol to find the silence he needed for composing. He demanded absolute quiet, retreating to a forest shack near a hamlet off the Pustertal. His Ninth Symphony and the uncompleted Tenth, written during those sessions amid the spruce and fir trees, may reflect the majesty of the Dolomite mountains around the narrow valley; the music surely betrays the angst in Mahler's mind.

Few Americans, oddly, know this sunny side of Europe's mountain spine more than superficially, although it is only a few hours by rail or car from Venice, Milan, or Munich and is traversed by major Continental north-south routes.

৵৹

MAY BATHS

I myself have spent long periods in every season in different corners of the region, and many people there have become my friends. The vernacular of my native Vienna is not too different from the Tyrolean dialect. As a longtime resident of Rome I can also connect and communicate easily with the Italians living in what to them is the Alto Adige. Some Ladins in the area have offered me hospitality. They speak a language that had its origin in the soldiers' Latin of the Roman legionnaires who occupied the Alpine provinces in 15 B.C. and garrisoned them until the sixth century. Ladin also contains words of the forgotten idiom of the Rhaetian tribes, recognizable in many place names throughout Tyrol and the Dolomites, and incorporates quite a few terms of the A.D. sixth-century Teutonic invaders and settlers. As a former foreign correspondent who reported to *The New York Times* from all continents, I have acquired enough material for comparison. I come back to South Tyrol and the Dolomites year after year; they are my favorite part of the world.

I had my first glimpses of southern Tyrol as a teenager, traveling home by train after a long hiking vacation in Italy. I was impressed by the rich green of the Alpine pastures, the cows gazing placidly at my train, the geraniums in the windows of many houses, and the high peaks on either side of the narrow valley through which the tracks ran up to the Brenner Pass. The train was pulled by two puffing steam locomotives and pushed by a third one at the rear. At the frontier station on the pass, the Italian locomotives were replaced by their Austrian counterparts. It was chilly, although we were at the height of summer.

In 1936 I spent a summer holiday in a town below the Brenner that was then officially known as Vipiteno, although the Tyroleans kept calling it by its centuries-old name, Sterzing. I had first heard of that place when making the acquaintance of a girl from there (she later became my wife). I had little money and had asked her to find me a very cheap inn. It was a little outside the town near a bridge across the Eisack River, which rises close to the Brenner Pass; the Italians called it the Isarco.

The inn's name was Maibad (May Baths). It was an old bathing establishment with three cabins containing tubs; local people came, especially on weekends, to soak in water that was heated in a central boiler. Sterzingers seem to have been convinced that the Maibad water, which came from a spring up the hillside beyond the raised railroad tracks, had special beneficial properties, although I couldn't find out which ones. In spa treatments, the important thing is the belief that the water is good for you. Nobody was able to tell me what the old bathing inn had to do with the month of May. Had the beginning of the Alpine spring once been the recommended time for a water cure?

There were also a few guest rooms. Mine was furnished with a creaking bed, a small table, a chair, and a dresser. The rough bedsheets smelled deliciously of the grass at the side of the river, where they had been laid out to dry after being laundered by hand.

The owner and manager of the inn was Luise, a short and peppery woman of local peasant stock who was also looking after what had remained of her family's nearby farm. When she became my landlady she was newly married (she was then in her thirties), and neighbors were still chuckling about her wedding trip. It seems Luise and Richard, her bumbling husband of a day, had intended to journey to the shrine of St. Anthony at Padua, whom Luise greatly revered; maybe they would also have proceeded to Venice. The couple, however, never got farther than Verona because Luise started pining for Rosl, her cow. Would her niece, Nannele, who had remained in charge of the baths and inn and the nearby stable, properly take care of the animal? Luise and her man returned from Verona to Sterzing on the next train, and she went straight from the station to see Rosl. The cow must have been pleased to be patted by its affectionate proprietress.

My fellow guests at the inn were traveling salesmen who would spend a night there after canvassing stores and prospective customers in town, and tourists on scanty budgets who were traveling the Brenner Road by motorcycle, bike, or on foot and who had learned of the inexpensive place, often by its listing in *Baedeker's Guide*.

One such transient was a young hitchhiker from northern Germany on his way to the South. After plopping his backpack on the bed that Luise had assigned to him, he washed up and went out for a night on the town. He returned in the morning, having had more of the cheap wine in some tavern than was good for him. While trying to find his way back to the inn, he had fallen into the Eisack River, fortunately just a trickle because there hadn't been a drop of rain for weeks and most of the snow on the mountains had melted. The German slept off his drunkenness on the escarpment, and when he showed up, bedraggled but unhurt, he said he didn't feel like having breakfast and just wanted to pick up his backpack and continue his journey. He didn't want to pay for his room, either, on the ground that he hadn't used it. "Oh, no!" Luise told him. "If you prefer to sleep in the river, that's your business. I gave you a room that somebody else might have taken, and you have to pay." He did, too.

In his typical fashion, Luise's husband stood by silently and seemed to sympathize with the hung-over hitchhiker. Richard was a mostly passive presence at the inn, heating the boiler, doing some work in the fields, and above all helping himself to the wine that Luise kept for guests in large bottles.

For dinner at the Maibad Inn there were usually only two choices. Luise would ask me, "Do you want a couple of eggs or a pair of frankfurters?" As a side order there was always crisp green salad from the kitchen garden, which ran up almost to the railroad tracks above the inn at a few yards' distance. I eventually got used to the noisy night trains to and from the Brenner Pass, which shook the entire inn as they rumbled by.

The battered but nevertheless cozy Maibad Inn was only a few minutes' walk from Sterzing's most ancient neighborhood. A footpath parallel to the river and the Brenner Road skirted a sloping pine grove before entering the Old Town. Somber medieval buildings huddled on either side of the cobblestone street, their broad doorways opening into dank interiors or into courtyards with wagons and horses. There were ripe smells. The Inn at the Sign of the Crown, on the right side of the Brenner Road (here called Old Town Street), had obviously been a resting place for many a weary traveler. When I first saw it, it was a hotel with only a few rooms and a tavern, and business seemed slack.

Old Town Street descended to Sterzing's Town Square and to the Black Eagle Restaurant and Hotel. When I saw the prices on the menu posted outside, I decided I couldn't afford it. My girlfriend and I listened to the music every time the municipal band gave a free concert in the square. Their bravura number was a medley from Rossini's *Guillaume Tell*.

✣

RENAISSANCE
COMPANY TOWN

From town square one entered the New Town—it was at least four hundred years old—through a passage of the clock tower known as Zwölferturm (Twelve O'Clock Tower). When noon was rung out from the terraced bell loft, businesses and offices all over the town closed, artisans put down their tools, and people got ready for lunch and maybe a snooze. The Mediterranean siesta habit also had a large following on the southern side of the Alps.

Sterzing's New Town, built after a devastating fire at the middle of the fifteenth century, was and still is today a delightful street lined with arcaded houses, many with bay windows; wrought-iron business signs jut out from the facades. It is the quintessential old Tyrolean main street, similar to those found in towns north of the Brenner. Gothic-style elements linger while Renaissance lines betray architectural influences from the south.

Coming from the Civic Tower, one sees Sterzing's Town Hall on the left side of the street. With its arcades, oriels, and battlemented flat roof, the building, erected 1468–75, is a little palazzo. When I was first in town an Italian official, named by the Fascist government in Rome instead of being elected by the local citizens, was running Vipiteno/Sterzing from the ancient Town Hall.

The title of the quasi-mayor was *podestà*, a word implying power (the Italian word for a popularly elected mayor is *sindaco*, but the term was then considered suspect). Sterzingers told me the *podestà* couldn't speak their language and didn't know what was going on in the town he was supposed to administer. I wasn't much interested in the way the Fascists were ruling the place, but several times I entered the courtyard of the Town Hall to puzzle out the significance of a stone relief apparently representing the killing of an ox by a man with a cape (or wings?) and a hood. An ancient bullfight?

Eventually a priest who had been on an errand in the Town Hall and saw me in the courtyard explained the relief to me. "This is a memorial of the pagan Mithras cult," he told me. "It's from the fourth century after the birth of Christ, and the stone was found three hundred and fifty years ago on a hill near Mauls in the Eisack Valley, south of here." According to archaeologists, the priest said, the relief showed the sacrifice of a bull by the god Mithras, and it may have been part of a shrine dedicated to that Near Eastern divinity. Mithras came to the Alps at about the same time as Christianity, both faiths being propagated by the legionaries of the Roman Empire. "Devotion to Mithras was fashionable among Roman soldiers for some time, but Jesus Christ in the end won out in Tyrol," the reverend said smugly.

The Roman legions marched up the Tyrolean Alps, commanded by Emperor Augustus's stepsons, Drusus and Tiberius, in 15 B.C., easily subjugating a population of mountaineers whom they called Rhaetians. The Romans garrisoned the area for centuries until the age of the barbarian invasions. During my many sojourns in the region in the years to come, I was to encounter quite a few supposed vestiges of the long submerged Rhaetian culture.

As a newcomer to Sterzing I quickly took to the local custom of strolling up and down the main street or under the arcades of the New Town late in the morning and again in the late afternoon whenever I wasn't exploring the side valleys and the nearby mountains. As during the daily *passeggiata* or *struscio* in more southerly Italian towns or the *paseo* ritual in Spain, people in Sterzing, at the appropriate hours, liked to see acquaintances and strangers, gossip, flirt a little, maybe, look into the shop windows, and take some refreshment as an occasion for human contact.

I noticed that the Italian espresso machine had conquered an important place in the old Tyrolean town south of the Brenner Pass; in northern Tyrol it was then still an exotic rarity. Four or five coffee bars on the main street were doing a brisk business. The Italian residents would sip their espresso or cappuccino standing at the counter, whereas Tyroleans preferred to drink theirs at little tables in the Austrian coffeehouse manner. Some of the older men kept asking for a glass of red wine, as they had always done, but younger Sterzingers had adopted the smart aperitif habit and took Italian vermouth, potent grappa, or *americano*, a cocktail containing vermouth and bitters with a dash of soda and a shred of lemon peel that was then the sophisticated drink.

The hotels in the New Town, like the Lamb and the Golden Cross, were heirs to old inns where such travelers as Goethe would spend the night during strenuous journeys down from the Brenner Pass. Now Italian army officers, assigned temporarily to the border area, took rooms in the hotels for their visiting wives or girlfriends.

Sterzing's parish church, Our Lady of the Wetlands, is a ten-minute walk from the New Town in a flat area that once must have been an often flooded near-bog. When I first entered the fifteenth-century Gothic edifice I was astonished by its grandeur. It looks like a bishop's cathedral, a reminder of the town's former importance and wealth.

When the big church went up, Sterzing was in fact a company town of the immensely rich Fugger family of Augsburg, which exploited silver and lead mines in the mountains in the Tyrolean town's vicinity. As Renaissance merchants and bankers, the house of Fugger traded with the Near East by way of Venice and granted loans to sovereigns, including the chronically cash-short Emperor Maximilian I. No wonder it was Maximilian, the "Last Knight," who obligingly laid the cornerstone of Sterzing's church.

Having read up on Sterzing before my first visit there, I was looking in the parish church for what was supposed to be one of South Tyrol's principal art treasures, an altarpiece by the Bavarian wood-carver and painter Hans Multscher, circa 1460. But only his sculpture of the Virgin Mary was there. The other parts of the artist's celebrated composition were known to be scattered in private collections and in safekeeping elsewhere. Later Mussolini would give a large portion of the Multscher altarpiece to the art-greedy Reich Marshall Hermann Göring. Much of the work has since then been recovered and can now be viewed in Sterzing's Multscher Museum (page 117).

ঞ

FORBIDDEN NAMES

In the cemetery behind the parish church the stonemasons had lately been busy. Tyrolean names on tombstones had to be changed into Italian-sounding ones; thus a long defunct Joseph Kollmann posthumously became Giuseppe Colma. The forced rechristening of dead people was to the Tyroleans a particularly rankling aspect of a broad program to Italianize the German-speaking territory that Italy had won from Austria at the end of World War I.

The name South Tyrol was outlawed, replaced by Alto Adige (Upper Adige). The Adige or, in German, Etsch is a river that rises in the northwest of the region, turns southward in a ninety-degree bend near the city of Bolzano, and rolls on to Trento, Verona, and the Adriatic Sea. The Isarco, or Eisack, is a tributary joining the Adige/Etsch a little below Bolzano.

In the same way as the region lost its historic name and Sterzing turned into Vipiteno, thousands of other towns, villages, hamlets, castles, monasteries, streams, rivers, torrents, mountains, hills, and diverse landmarks had been relabeled. A geographer and Italian nationalist who was a member of the Rome parliament, Senator Count Ettore Tolomei from Rovereto (1865–1952) furnished almost all of the new names. At times he was able to find an appropriate Latin term (like Vipitenum) in old texts. In many other instances he invented new Italian names on the basis of assonance or other criteria: the villages of Völs and Burgstall, for example, became Fiè and Postal; the towns of Toblach and Glurns found themselves called Dobbiaco and Glorenza; and the Jaufen Pass near Sterzing was to be known as the Passo del Giovo. The town of Bruneck was renamed Brunico, but Italians themselves are to this day unsure whether to stress the first or the second syllable.

The new Fascist authorities sought to eradicate lingering reminiscences and loyalties also in other ways. My future mother-in-law, whose husband had died as an Austrian soldier during World War I, told me that several years earlier carabinieri had burst into her modest home and torn a picture of Emperor Franz Joseph off the wall. If a portrait of old, bewhiskered Franz Joseph, dead for two decades, or any other reminder of former Austria-Hungary was found, there would be trouble. Gangs of Fascists beat up young Tyroleans wearing white stockings to their leather breeches, a clothing style interpreted as an anti-Italian demonstration.

School in Sterzing was all Italian. My girlfriend Maria had learned to sing *"Giovinezza, Giovinezza!"* ("Youth, Youth!"), the Fascist hymn. She spoke the Tyrolean dialect as her first language, was fluent in Italian, but had never learned standard German. Most Tyroleans in Sterzing were similarly bilingual to a degree; they had to be because all business in Town Hall, in the courthouse, at the tax office, and at the railroad station had to be transacted in Italian. Many Italian officials had come from the deep south or Sicily, and very few ever learned German. One who did was a Sicilian carabinieri sergeant of many years' service in Sterzing. He married a local girl, passably spoke the Tyrolean dialect, and was generally liked. He would stay on in town after his retirement.

During my month in Sterzing I found that the local people, especially when they had one glass too many of their red wine, might mutter about their current masters but in general tried to make the best of the situation and get along with the Italians. Tyroleans weren't like the Irish or the Basques. The last time they had rebelled was in 1809, when the mountaineers rose up against Napoleon and his Bavarian allies, defeated one of his generals, and eventually were themselves beaten into submission.

From the old Hapsburg monarchy the Tyroleans had inherited a tradition of respect for authority. The young men of Sterzing obediently, if dejectedly, left for Florence, Naples, or Sardinia when they were called up for military service. Local girls took up with Italian army officers and functionaries, and there were quite a few interethnic marriages, although many people in town and especially on the mountainsides disapproved of them.

On the surface I could detect little tension. The atmosphere in Sterzing seemed pleasant, and I heard a lot of joking and laughter. Young Tyrolean women served as nursemaids for the children of Italian officials who, with their families, lived in gracelessly utilitarian houses that the Fascist government had erected for them near the New Town. Bleak army barracks had gone up on the outskirts.

The Tyrolean shopkeepers and property owners in town considered themselves *Bürger* (burghers) and looked down on the military personnel, policemen, and bureaucrats whom the Fascist government in Rome had sent them. The newcomers had to live on skimpy salaries in rented apartments and had to spend their money at the local baker's and butcher's. There were almost no Italian-owned shops in town.

Only on Saturdays Italian merchants from the Trentino, Friuli, and Veneto regions showed up for the weekly market with their trucks and trailers, offering meat, groceries, fruits, wine, shoes, apparel, cutlery, and tools and providing competition to the smug "burgher" shopkeepers. Farmers came down from the mountains and bargained spiritedly with the salespeople at the outdoor market for a pair of boots or a newfangled agricultural utensil. Many of the market vendors sported the same bib aprons of blue denim that the Tyrolean peasants and craftsmen were wearing like a uniform. The mountain farmers seemed to have an unspoken understanding with the traders from the Trentino, Friuli, and Veneto in sniffing at the southern Italians in town.

Actually, Sterzing, then with a resident population of four thousand, was living to a considerable degree off the Italian army, police, and civilians that Rome had stationed in the strategic area below the Brenner Pass. International transit business and tourism brought in little money then. The mass-travel industry was just starting, and it was still an event when a tourist coach stopped in the town square.

I soon became aware that the Tyroleans of Sterzing had been far more profoundly influenced by eighteen years of Italian rule than they themselves realized. They had learned to like spaghetti, gelato, and espresso. When my girlfriend and I wanted to see a movie, we had to go to the ugly new building of the Fascist leisure organization Dopolavoro; off-duty soldiers and young Tyroleans both would laugh at the jokes of Italian film comedies or Italian-dubbed imports.

Many Italian expressions had crept into the Southern Tyroleans' speech. They said *merenda* instead of *Jause* when they meant an afternoon snack and moaned *"I bin stuff"* for "I am sick and tired" (there is no such German word as *stuff*—it's the Italian *stufo*, fed up). Tyrolean women, especially the wives and daughters of "burghers," copied the fashions of Italian officers' wives and began to wear the cork-soled "orthopedic" shoes that were then becoming the rage in Italy.

Despite such cultural osmosis there was little love between Tyroleans and Italians except for those cases of individual romance and marriage. Some Tyrolean girls I met had their fun on week-ends, dropping in at the railway station to watch the emotional scenes—all that hugging and kissing, those shouts of "Mamma!"—when members of Italian families were arriving or leaving. South Tyroleans, convinced to be made of sterner stuff, derided such demonstrative behavior. They didn't know then that they themselves were already being criticized by Northern Tyroleans as showy and effeminate near-Latins.

A young Sterzing upholsterer, Hans, who professed to hate Italians and who disseminated little swastika emblems among his friends, was at the same time a fan of the tenor Beniamino Gigli and couldn't hear enough of his records with Verdi and Puccini arias and his hit song "Mamma!"

Some young people, like Hans, were Nazis. Hitler's rise in Germany had filled them with giddy hopes that he would eventually get them, together with the Austrians, into his Third Reich. Didn't the German national anthem in the text by the chauvinistic wordsmith August Heinrich Hoffmann von Fallersleben define the nation as comprising all territory "from the Etsch to the Belt," that is, from South Tyrol's main river to the Baltic Sea?

That summer, however, the local Nazis were dispirited. Mussolini, having lost Western sympathies because of his aggression on Ethiopia, was veering closer to Germany. Hitler appeared glad to welcome his fellow dictator as a full-fledged ally; the Pact of Steel was being forged, implying German acquiescence in the status quo south of the Brenner, where the Tyrolean-German-speaking population were no more numerous than the residents of just one city district of Munich.

&

ARCHAIC WORLD

But of course I hadn't come to analyze South Tyrol's social and political conditions and international status. Instead, advised and often guided by my girlfriend, I discovered the town's beautiful surroundings. Sterzing is at 3,110 feet (948) meters altitude, and mornings were cool, although that August was exceptionally hot. When the sun was high I often was already on the top of the 7,181-foot (2,189-meter) Rosskopf (Horse's Head), which overlooks the town, or on some other nearby peak or ridge. Maria showed me mountain paths that she had climbed since she was a little girl.

Sterzing is situated near the openings of four side valleys from which streams join the Eisack River. Some of the villages and hamlets all around have ancient names that sound neither German nor Italian and appear to be residues of the forgotten Rhaetian language—like Pflersch, Ridnaun, Tschöfs (Senator Tolomei had Italianized them too into Fleres, Ridanna, and Ceves). I trekked to many of them on foot or on a borrowed bicycle. I had borrowed also a windbreaker, which I would take off and put on again as the weather changed; on a hot day an icy wind might suddenly sweep down from the glaciers in the north or dark clouds would move in from the west but race farther eastward to discharge a thunderstorm in the Dolomites or in Carinthia.

What I saw on the slopes was an archaic world where people worked astonishingly hard and lived on a little agriculture and, principally, as cattle breeders. That hot summer almost all of the cows were up on the grassland on top of the mountains. To see such an alp I would climb paths that had in all likeliness been trod by prehistoric settlers, up ravines and across dense forests of oaks, pines, and larches until the trees became smaller and fewer and eventually ended at around 6,000 feet (2,000 meters) above sea level, at expanses of short grass between rocky outcrops.

On such an alp a cowherd would live a solitary life all summer, taking care, with assistance from an alert dog, of the cattle entrusted to him. The bells of the older cows were tinkling from morning to night as the herd was grazing, the main job of the cowherd and his dog being to prevent the animals from straying too far and maybe coming to harm in some crevasse. The cowherd's hut and food were primitive. Now and then he would get fresh bread, some lard and cheese, and wine from the valley, but there was always plenty of milk from the cows. Cowherds were always glad to have somebody to talk to.

They told me they were looking forward to the glorious day when they would drive their herd down to the winter stables, the coats of the animals glistening with health, the horns of the lead cows decorated with Alpine flowers. I wouldn't see the return of the cattle to the valleys that time, but later I was often witness to that Alpine autumn parade and every time feeling strangely stirred by the apparent solemnity of the animals, with their deliberate gait and the sound of their bells, and the dogs looking self-consciously important. It is a scene that has been enacted annually in the mountains for thousands of years. Now it usually holds up motor traffic on the roads in the valleys.

Climbing over the stiles of cattle fences the way Maria had taught me, I would reach a farmstead that was 4,500 feet (1,500 meters) above sea level or even higher. The buildings were often twinned—a broad stonework house, usually two stories high, in which the farm family lived under a sloping roof would be adjoined by a wooden stable and hayloft of about the same height. Flaming geraniums and yolky marigolds in the windows provided friendly tufts of color. There might be a kitchen garden nearby, surrounded by a high wire fence to keep out the deer, which would come out of the forests at dawn and loved to breakfast on the salad and cabbage the farmer's wife was growing. Each solitary farmhouse on the mountains was a self-sufficient family enterprise, because in winter it might be snowed in and cut off from the valley for weeks.

That summer the people in the mountains had little time to talk to me: they were busy haying on the steep slopes for the second time in the season because the torrid heat that had prevailed for weeks might any day be broken by thunderstorms that would drench and spoil the cut grass laid out to dry. Almost all of the grass cutting was then still done with scythes and sickles.

Hardly any mountain farm was employing hired labor; everybody in the family pitched in. It was a small, closed, patriarchal society that also included the domestic animals. When the owner died, his oldest son or another relative would go around the stables and announce to the cattle, horses, sheep, goats, pigs, and chickens: "The farmer is dead!"

The oldest son would be the sole heir to the entire property. Under age-old Tyrolean customary law, codified by Empress Maria Theresa in the eighteenth century, the defunct farmer's other children might stay on as laborers or ask to be paid off if there was enough money, but they couldn't claim any portion of the building, the livestock, or the land. The mountain farmsteads were indivisible, and most of them remained so also under Italian rule. Even Mussolini didn't dare introduce Roman inheritance law in the South Tyrolean mountains, because the consequence of subdivisions over two or three generations would have been bedsheet-size plots, meaning the end of Alpine farming.

The system of the "closed" mountain farm or, as the Italians call it, the *maso chiuso*, is harsh on the siblings of the sole heir, but it has saved the economy of high-altitude cattle breeding to this day. The Fascist regime in its attempts to Italianize the region settled peasants from the south on its slopes whenever some property became available; all those experiments failed. Hill farmers from Tuscany or Calabria who were thus transplanted to the Alpine areas gave up after a few frustrating years, during which they were cold-shouldered by the Tyroleans, were appalled by the rough winters and the loneliness, and despite tax abatements failed to make any profits.

The names of the Tyrolean farmers as recorded in the parish registers of births, marriages, and deaths often were—and still are today—different from the names by which they were and are generally known. The old appellation of the farmstead, which over hundreds of years may have been taken over by a married daughter or some other family, is transferred to its new owners. Thus someone whose personal documents identify him as Josef (or Giuseppe) Kofler was and is called by everybody the Ried Bauer (Ried Farmer) or the Ried Josef or Sepp.

Maria and I would sometimes buy a snack at a farmhouse after a tiring climb. Cash was always welcome, and the farmer's wife would give us chunks of bread she had baked herself, delicious sour milk, and thick slices of *Speck* for an amount of lire that to me seemed ridiculously small. *Speck* is a Tyrolean treat (page 211); in its genuine form, nowadays increasingly hard to get, it is ham and lard that has been smoke-cured in a farmhouse chimney over months.

What struck me during my hikes around Sterzing was the great number of churches, chapels, little wayside shrines, and crossroad crucifixes. There seemed to be some Roman Catholic place of worship in the tiniest hamlet, and needle-shaped steeples of churches and chapels stuck out of what from the valley looked like dense forest. On each trip I passed a dozen little wooden or stone outdoor sanctuaries adorned by images of the Virgin Mary or some saint, wooden crosses with carvings of an agonizing Jesus, and almost always fresh flowers. The Church of Rome had since the early Middle Ages maintained a powerful hold over this section of the Alps and in some measure still does at present.

Several times I ran into what even I, then completely innocent of any military experience, recognized as camouflaged fortifications. A bulbous mass looking like a bizarre outcrop might hang over a road in a gorge; if I examined it more closely, I noticed that the seeming rock was artificial, and I could discern slits in it that were plugged embrasures. It was an unmanned bunker, its entrance concealed, and local people said it had been built quite recently. A few such strongholds were being completed in the vicinity even then, I learned, but I never saw any actual fortification work going on. The story was that Mussolini didn't trust the Germans and was securing Italy's northern frontier against a possible invasion even while he was negotiating with Hitler about concluding a formal military alliance.

Oddly, Mussolini's Alpine fortification program would continue through most of World War II. Though Italy might have used the financial, material, and manpower resources that it swallowed more rationally for the war effort elsewhere, one explanation would be that Mussolini feared the Nazis might eventually try to snatch South Tyrol after the hypothetical victory of the Berlin-Rome Axis. A more cynical theory would be that greedy

contractors in a conspiracy with Fascist bigwigs and corrupt generals kept pouring concrete into mountain gullies simply because
the necessary funds had been appropriated by the government
and the payoffs had been made.

A cluster of disguised bunkers flanked the Brenner Road
where it passed a ravine less than a mile north of the Maibad
Inn, and my landlady told me that when they were being built
the workers often came to wash up in her place and drink her
wine. "If there's a war, we'll be on the front line here," Luise's
husband, Richard, said darkly. "Holy Mother of God," Luise
moaned. "We must get Rosl out." She was worrying about
her cow.

After a month at the Maibad Inn I was hooked on the sunny
side of the Alps, although I knew only a small patch of the region.
I hadn't yet seen the cold mountain lakes, the high plateau of
the Seis/Siusi Alp with its millions of flowers in May, or the
dramatic veined rock towers of the Dolomites, which glow when
the sun sets. Nor had I beheld the vineyards of the Wine Road
or the orchards of the broad Vinschgau/Val Venosta. I hadn't
visited Bolzano or the other major towns of the province or any
of its many castles, except Reifenstein and Sprechenstein on two
hills framing Sterzing. I would return often to catch up with what
I had missed.

❧

A PILGRIMAGE

Almost thirty years after my first visit and many subsequent vacations in various parts of the region, I put up again at the Maibad
Inn. I was then chief of the Madrid bureau of *The New York*

Times and for months had attended diplomatic dinners, stayed at Seville's Alfonso XIII, Lisbon's Ritz, and other fancy hotels around Spain and Portugal, eaten paella in Valencia, and listened to flamenco in Malaga and fado singers in Coimbra. It was time, I felt, to revert to a simpler life for a while.

The old name Sterzing, twinned with the Italian one, Vipiteno, had been restored at the town's railroad station. The region was officially bilingual now (soon to become trilingual as Ladin would be recognized by the authorities). The Maibad Inn still shook every time one of the many passenger and freight trains passed on the tracks on the slope above it, though they were now pulled by one powerful electric engine rather than by three steam locomotives.

Luise's place had undergone a face-lift. The former bathing cabins with their iron tubs had been converted into modern bathrooms for guests. Most people in town had their own bathrooms, and nobody came to Luise's establishment for a hot soak anymore. For dinner, sure enough, you could still order eggs or franks, but Nannele, the owner's niece, could also produce schnitzel on request. The salad from the kitchen garden was still a treat to look forward to. Luise no longer had a cow but still spoke lovingly of Rosl, who had long gone to cattle heaven. Richard was still taking care of the boiler and of his wife's wine bottles.

Dinner was late one night because Luise with her husband and her niece had undertaken a pilgrimage on foot to the shrine of Maria Trens, a church in a hamlet a few miles south of Sterzing that treasures a late-Gothic image of the Virgin Mary, represented as wearing a red-and-gold cape and red shoes with golden soles. It is supposed to be working miracles. People from neighboring towns and farmers from the hillsides will trek to Maria Trens to pray for recovery from sickness, the return of a faithless lover, or dry weather until the hay and the fruits are brought in.

The interior walls of the church are covered with naive votive pictures showing small children being rescued from drowning in the Eisack River, cattle spared by lightning, and soldiers coming back from the war with only an arm missing. My wife's sister-in-law had dragged herself on her knees all the way from the Brenner Road to the church, about half a mile (eight hundred meters), to fulfill a vow when her husband returned unhurt from World War II. She had promised the Madonna of Trens to do such penitence if she ever saw him again alive.

Over the years my wife and I must have taken the pleasant stroll from Vipiteno/Sterzing to Maria Trens and back on at least a dozen Sunday afternoons—for relaxation rather than because of religious fervor. With us, usually, were her older sister Julia, the latter's husband, Mariano, who was an Italian army officer, and their little girls. Mariano had seen action in Ethiopia, had been made a prisoner of war by the British, and had been sent to India, where he was held in a camp for years. After repatriation he was assigned to an army command in Bolzano. He never learned more than a few words of German but was well liked by the Tyroleans. On our Sunday outings during the 1950s Mariano wore not his major's uniform, but a double-breasted city suit with a necktie, while everyone else in the restaurant garden where we had snacks was dressed casually.

Most casual was also Luise's pilgrimage many years later, whose tail end I witnessed. She and her fellow devotees implored the Virgin Mary in the church to procure I don't know which heavenly favor and afterward partook of refreshments in the shadowy garden of the old Bircher Inn that is conveniently close to the sanctuary. They must have had a good time because they started their march home much later than they had planned and apparently were a little fatigued. A few acquaintances whom they had met at Maria Trens went with them.

When the group at last reached the Maibad Inn, Richard invited everybody to another glass of wine, and Luise's kitchen filled up with convivial people. Nannele remembered that paying guests were waiting for dinner in the adjoining room and inquired what we wanted to eat. Schnitzel and salad would be just fine, we told her.

Nannele returned a few minutes later to ask me to come to the telephone—somebody was calling in a language she couldn't understand; would I mind finding out what or whom he wanted?

The inn's only phone was in the kitchen. When I entered I saw Luise, her husband, and their guests at a table with glasses of red wine before them while Nannele went back to the range to fry our schnitzels. The noise was considerable, and I could hardly hear the voice speaking out of the phone. It was in English, came from New York, and belonged to Clifton E. Daniel, President Truman's son-in-law and, at the time, managing editor of *The New York Times*. "Sorry to interrupt what sounds like a yodeling party," Daniel said. He had once been a foreign correspondent in Switzerland and wasn't far off in his acoustic guess.

My trip to the South Tyrol was quickly cut short—I'd been called to reopen the Havana bureau at once. I had just enough time to eat Nannele's schnitzel with my wife before taking the night train. Spouses of foreign correspondents become used to sudden departures and long separations. I wasn't surprised at all that Daniel had called the Maibad Inn. "They'll find you anywhere, especially during your time off," is what reporters say of their home office.

Six months later I continued my South Tyrolean vacation, though not at the Maibad Inn. After the heat in Castro's island I relished the bracing Alpine air. Since then I have gone back to South Tyrol and the Dolomites at various times every year.

❧

PROSPEROUS
MOUNTAIN PROVINCE

Today, as I am writing these lines, I am in the Gherdëina Valley looking out on a green slope across a stream that local people call "the brook," although it may turn into a raging torrent. I have returned, again, to the South Tyrol. Some 900 feet (300 meters) above me is a farmhouse whose inhabitants I know; they speak Ladin among themselves. They keep cows in a tall wooden stable and barn to the left of their home. Last week I watched them toiling on the steep meadow below their house as they were hurrying to bundle and bring in the hay—just in time, too, because a hailstorm came down that evening. It was a Sunday, and the younger members of the family were able to help. On weekdays a son and two daughters drive to jobs in the nearby town of Urtijëi (officially called Ortisei in Italian and St. Ulrich in German), leaving their elders to cope with the farmwork, the cows, pigs, and chickens. Above their farm rise the dark evergreen forests of the 7,503-foot (2,282-meter) Raschötz mountain, its uppermost 600 feet (200 meters) covered only with sparse grassland.

The farmers on the slope across the stream are well off. They take paying guests—Italian families with children in summer and skiers in winter—in two rooms that they have had cozily wainscoted and equipped with bathrooms and television. They furnish milk to the local dairy cooperative and use new agricultural machines. They drive a car, a pickup truck, a motorbike, and two motor scooters. And they work hard. One of the daughters is a bank teller when she doesn't help out on the farm, the other is waitressing seasonally in an Urtijëi hotel, and the son fills up cars and does small repairs at a service station.

The laboriousness of the people is one reason mountain farming has survived south of the Brenner Pass. Other important factors are winter sports and summer tourism, both of which bring in much cash. Light industries like mechanical, optical, and furniture factories that have sprung up on the outskirts of some towns provide many jobs, but quite a few of their workers and employees still help out on family farms. Almost everybody has agricultural roots. South Tyrol comes closer to full employment of the resident population, at least during some months of the year, than most other areas in Italy.

The manifest prosperity is also due to the absence of any major ethnic conflicts. This doesn't mean that the German-speaking and Italian-speaking people in the region particularly like each other; they just have learned to get along. The small Ladin minority is friendly with both major groups while culturally feeling closer to the Tyroleans than to the Italians.

When they are among themselves the South Tyroleans more often than not speak of their Italian fellow citizens as *Walsche*. The term is kindred to the English word *Welsh* and carries overtones of disparagement, as in the English verb *to welsh*. Italians, on the other hand, when they aren't overheard by Tyroleans, call them *crucchi*, a nickname conveying a sense of stodginess and primitivity. It is derived from the Serbo-Croatian word *kruh* (bread), by which Italian soldiers during World War I used to refer first to the

Croatians and other southern Slavs among the Austrian-Hungarian forces and eventually also to German-speaking enemy troops.

To Italians today the quintessential *crucchi* are the *Schützen* (marksmen), who in their folklore costumes parade again, without any weapons, in South Tyrolean towns and villages on festive occasions. They are members of a loose, conservative organization of volunteers who consider themselves heirs to the traditions of the former Tyrolean militia. Under the Fascist regime the *Schützen* were outlawed, but they kept in touch clandestinely. At present a few *Schützen* "companies" are also active in Ladin towns and in the Italian-speaking province of Trento.

Post-Fascist Italy, in a deal with Austria, granted the provinces of Bolzano and Trento, both of which had belonged to Austria-Hungary, a measure of autonomy in administrative matters and recognized the right of the local populations to use their maternal languages in dealings with the authorities. Since then the relations between the two major ethnic communities in the area went through periods of trouble. During the 1960s Tyrolean extremists bombed some monuments that Fascist Italy had erected in their region as well as high-tension pylons of the state-controlled power company. There were few casualties. Some of the terrorism that occurred during those years, then attributed to Tyrolean plotters, was later found to have been engineered by the Italian secret services for Macchiavellian reasons of their own.

During the 1980s interethnic relations improved markedly as the region was experiencing something of an economic boom, and most people in the mixed-language territory realized it was in their common interest to do business together. In 1992 the parliament in Vienna voted a motion acknowledging that the government in Rome had fulfilled all the terms of the Austrian-Italian treaty of 1946, which created a special status for South

Tyrol, and of the subsequent accords regarding the area. This "victory of reasonableness" south of the Brenner Pass was sealed at just the time when former Yugoslavia, only a few hundred miles to the east, was convulsed by outbreaks of old tribal and religious hatreds. International observers cited the achievement of ethnic peace in the Tyrolean Alps as a model for the solution of similar conflicts in less fortunate parts of the continent.

Today about two-thirds of the 440,000 inhabitants of the autonomous province of Bolzano/Südtirol, a mountain area less than a third the size of Vermont, are German-speaking; not quite a third are ethnic Italians; and fewer than 5 percent belong to the Ladin group. The province has its own parliament and government, enacts its own laws, and wields considerable bureaucratic powers. German-speaking South Tyrolean senators and deputies sit in the national parliament in Rome. In exchange for the taxes that the province pays to the Italian treasury, it receives sizable funds from Rome, enabling it to subsidize mountain farming, finance ambitious public work programs like the construction of low-rent public housing and the harnessing of Alpine torrents, and pay indemnities to peasants and property owners after devastating storms or in other emergencies. Lately the province has also become responsible for maintaining some of the national highways on its territory.

Elected representatives of the German-speaking population enjoy a majority in the provincial parliament, and German-speaking officials dominate the province's government and administrative machinery. Italian residents keep complaining that they suffer discrimination in the assignment of public-housing apartments, in hiring for provincial offices, and in other respects. As a general rule, jobs in the provincial bureaucracy and other plums are to be allotted according to the statistical proportion of the three ethnic groups. In practice, quite a few people who at home speak Italian or Ladin declare themselves German-speaking to the census takers and in job applications to qualify for public employment.

South Tyrol's ruling German-speaking politicians do not seem to favor integration between the local Italians and the majority of the province's population. German-language and Italian-language schools are strictly separated, although the nonmaternal tongue is taught a few hours every week. Many more German-speaking South Tyroleans are also fluent in Italian than the other way around. Italians, especially visitors from other parts of the nation, resent what they call the apartheid in the province of Alto Adige/Südtirol. Although the two major ethnic communities don't mind making money together, there is little social and cultural contact between them. Yet Italian-speaking natives of the area appear quite content with such separateness, joining in the widespread prosperity, and show no desire to move farther to the south of the country, where only Italian is spoken.

Since the late 1980s the ethnic climate in South Tyrol has changed perceptibly as a result of new patterns in its all-important tourist business. For many years Germans were predominant among the area's vacation guests; on the highest mountain roads one was sure to encounter many Mercedeses with Hamburg and Munich license plates. Lately the number of Germans visiting South Tyrol has remained static or even decreased as Italians from other provinces discover the sunny side of the Alps. Disgust with sea pollution off long stretches of the Italian coastline and other ecological woes play a role in the recent vogue of verdant Alto Adige/South Tyrol among Italian holiday makers. Italians from other parts of the nation have also learned to appreciate the relative absence of crime, the general neatness, and the efficiency of public services in the northern territory. German-speaking South

Tyroleans and Ladins, in turn, welcome the Italian guests who are generally known to splurge during vacations and try to meet their tastes.

Spaghetti, ravioli, and lasagne appear more frequently on hotel and restaurant menus, and the only television set in small pensions seems permanently tuned in to Italian-language channels. Farmers and villagers who meet Italian-looking strangers on some mountain path will greet them with a polite *"Buon giorno!"*

✌

OVERDEVELOPMENT

During the 1950s Italy built a motorway linking the nation's principal north-south road axis—the Autostrada del Sole (Motor Road of the Sun), or A-1—with the Brenner Pass from Modena by way of Verona, Trento, and Bolzano. This Autostrada del Brennero (Motor Road of the Brenner Pass), or A-22, continues from the Austrian-Italian frontier as A-13 to Innsbruck, the capital of the Austrian Region of Tyrol. Shortly before reaching Innsbruck, not quite 25 miles (40 kilometers) to the north of the Brenner, the road passes the Europa Bridge, which is 2,624 feet (800 meters) long and at 591 feet (180 meters) above the floor of the valley one of the continent's loftiest viaducts.

In addition to the heavy, and steadily increasing, international traffic between northern Europe and Italy, there is also much traveling between North and South Tyrol across the Brenner. Young South Tyroleans study at Innsbruck University (which includes an Institute of Italian Law) or other Austrian schools, and South Tyrolean patients seek treatment in Innsbruck clinics. People from North Tyrol, conversely, make frequent trips south of the Brenner, especially on weekends, also because wine and fruits are cheaper there than at home.

Environmentalists lament that the broad concrete ribbon of the Brenner motorway has violated the landscape of the Adige/ Etsch and Isarco/Eisack Valleys and attracted additional traffic that otherwise would have to be absorbed by the old two-lane Brenner Road and the Brenner rail line. On the other hand, A-22, bypassing the historic centers of major towns as well as several ancient villages, has saved them from further congestion. As the volume of north-south traffic is continually expanding, Italian, Austrian, and German engineers are discussing the project of a long railroad tunnel below the Brenner Pass, which would speed train service between Bolzano and Innsbruck and lighten the burden that the roads have to bear at present.

Since the opening of the A-22 motorway, South Tyrol has become a prime area for winter sports and year-round recreation. Roads into the side valleys and up the mountains were widened and asphalted, and new ones were built; funiculars, chair lifts, and T-lifts sprouting almost everywhere enable non-Alpinists and skiers to reach the peaks and pistes effortlessly; hotels, pensions, and rooms for rent are proliferating; and ever new facilities for leisure activities and fun are being created.

For example, the town of Urtijëi/Ortisei/St. Ulrich, a gateway to the Dolomites, has at the time of writing a permanent population of 4,500 and offers nearly 3,000 guest beds in hotels and pensions plus several hundred rooms for short-term rent in private homes. The Ladin center boasts a modern convention building, a year-round ice-skating rink and stadium, a public bathing establishment with an Olympic-size indoor pool and outdoor pools, a tennis and squash complex with open-air and indoor courts, and a horse-riding school. Several hotels have outdoor and indoor swimming pools, saunas, and fitness rooms. Nine funiculars and chair lifts in the immediate surroundings take skiers and summer visitors to the heights. A mountaineering school trains would-be Alpinists and provides licensed mountain guides. In town a guest may choose among two dozen restaurants, cafes, and pizzerias and a couple of discotheques. For shopping, there are a supermarket and an array of stores and boutiques.

Many other towns and villages in the region offer similar possibilities for accommodation, exercise, and relaxation. Thousands of young people descend from the hillsides and the isolated mountain farms during the peak tourist seasons in winter and summer to take service jobs in the valleys.

Ecologists have for years warned that the sunny side of the Alps is threatened by overdevelopment. Three-car families are now no rarity among the local population. This—and the invasion by motorized tourists every year—in addition to the constant commercial traffic in the main valleys have brought air pollution and are endangering the forests by acid rain. For really clean air you have to climb to altitudes above 4,500 feet (about 1,500 meters).

Despite the roaring tourist industry, however, the traditional mountain economy has so far held out. Go up the unpaved roads and paths off the highways almost anywhere in the area, especially in the side valleys, and you will reach lofty hamlets and lonely farmsteads where the ancient, toilsome way of life doesn't seem to have changed much. The mountaineers still go about their annual cycle of labors—tending cattle, haying, and tackling their many other chores. True, they now use tractors instead of oxen and wield the scythes and sickles only on the steepest grassland. Television shortens their winter evenings, and when the roads are passable the farmers go to town by car to shop.

On the lower hillsides vintages are grown that according to Italian wine critics are now among the nation's best. The broad valleys south and west of Bolzano have become plantations producing choice apples, pears, apricots, peaches, plums, and table grapes.

The supremely scenic Dolomites are geographically an appendage to South Tyrol, but their character is much more Italian. The area, long inaccessible, belonged for hundreds of years to the Republic of Venice before it became Austrian and remained so until World War I; the local idiom is Friulan, which is related to Ladin. Administratively, much of the Dolomites is today a part of the province of Belluno and the Veneto region, but in their main town, Cortina d'Ampezzo, one of Italy's most fashionable resorts, some local politicians advocate joining the autonomous province of Bolzano/Südtirol to win greater independence from the central government in Rome and share in the relative well-being of the neighboring province. (For more information on the Dolomites, see chapter 8.)

Environmental lobbies in both South Tyrol and the Dolomites have lately gained strength. They keep denouncing air and water pollution and are fighting projects envisaging more asphalt and concrete roads; funiculars and ski lifts; hotels and chalets; golf courses and other sports installations; and service stations. One can only hope that these Green movements succeed in preventing the area from being transmogrified into an Alpine theme park.

Severe regulations already protect the wildlife and vegetation in the region, and they seem effective. Even on the outskirts of major towns deer will come down from the forests in the early morning hours and occasionally in the evenings during the warm months to forage and even to venture crossing the main roads. Signs showing the outline of a jumping roe warn motorists to watch out for such adventurous animals. In winter, hungry deer approach the mountain farms to pick up handouts. Alpinists in the Dolomites near Cortina d'Ampezzo often see chamois leaping nimbly from rock to rock.

Visitors may obtain temporary hunting or fishing licenses (see page 207). Mushroom-picking is restricted in some parts of the territory and prohibited in others because fungi are an essential part of the Alpine biosphere and nourishment for the animals. Various Alpine flowers are protected, meaning that it is illegal to pluck even only one specimen. Among these is the edelweiss ("noble white"), a humble plant with velvety white flowers that grows spontaneously only at high altitudes; the potted edelweiss offered by florists is an inferior variety that may be freely bought. The edelweiss is also the emblem of the region's strongest political force, the Südtiroler Volkspartei (South Tyrolean People's Party), which for decades had a near-monopoly as representation of the German-speaking and Ladin population but lately has been challenged by Greens and other movements. The flowers in many windows and on the balconies that struck me during my first trip across South Tyrol many years ago and the gorgeousness of private gardens and public parks keep enhancing the charms of the verdant valleys and slopes.

II.

THE ICEMAN

❧

M ount Similaun, 11,817 feet (3,602 meters) above sea level, is one of the highest peaks along the main crest of the Alps between Austria and Italy. If there isn't too much snow, it presents no difficulties to experienced climbers, although to reach its summit to enjoy a grandiose panorama they will have to traverse glacier fields and crevasses.

The vast glaciers of the Similaun have been imperceptibly creeping around the slopes and clefts below the peak ever since the Ice Age. In 1991 at the end of an exceptionally warm Alpine summer the Similaun's melting ice yielded the mummified body of a person. Quickly dubbed *Homo tyrolensis* (Tyrolean Man), he was pronounced the world's oldest nearly intact human being.

The find, with its bow, quiver, arrows, copper ax, flint dagger, and other equipment, proved to anthropologists that central Europeans in the younger Stone Age possessed a much higher degree of technological sophistication than had until then been assumed. To Tyroleans it was additional evidence that people had been living in their high mountains a very long time. *Homo tyrolensis* became a subject of ethnic pride.

Curiously, the section of the Alps including Mount Similaun was the scene of another scientific sensation sixty years earlier.

The peak is a little less than 10 miles (16 kilometers) southwest of Obergurgl, which at 6,256 feet (1,907 meters) altitude is Austria's highest village; near that lofty settlement the Swiss professor Auguste Piccard landed on a glacier in May 1931 after having for the first time ascended to the stratosphere in a balloon designed by himself. In a way it was the start of space exploration.

The Iceman of the Similaun—the "oldest Tyrolean"—was first sighted by two German tourists, Helmut Simon, a fifty-four-year-old employee of the Nuremberg Civic Library, and his wife, Erika. The couple were walking down from the summit, where they had admired and photographed the vistas on a clear day, September 19, 1991; at about 10,500 feet (3,200 meters) altitude they walked around a little pond that melting snow and ice had formed. It was then that they spotted the head and shoulders of what they first thought was a dressmaker's dummy or a large doll thrown away by a child. Discarded toys, soft-drink cans, plastic bags, and other garbage, alas, clutter many scenic sites in the Alps today, but there is no cableway or chair lift all the way up to the Similaun peak, and it seemed unlikely that anyone would climb with a child or a life-size doll to a high glacier.

Mrs. Simon was first to realize that what they were seeing was a dead person. The couple walked closer and, on noticing the body's brown, leathery skin with the skeleton outlined clearly underneath, concluded that death must have occurred a considerable time earlier. Mr. Simon took a picture, and he and his wife continued their descent to the Similaun Refuge at 9,988 feet (3,047 meters) altitude. The Simons told the shelter's manager of their grisly find, proceeded to the valley, and three days later returned home.

The Similaun Refuge, which is on Italian territory, is in

summer a veritable mountain inn with beds and bunks. Its young manager, Markus Pirpamer, called the carabinieri station in the Schnals Valley/Val Senales at the foot of the Similaun to report what the German tourists had said to have seen. The narrow Schnals Valley has long become a winter sports area popular with Italian skiers, but the carabinieri knew that a major portion of Mount Similaun is in Austria and that people who climb it are mostly Austrians, Belgians, Dutch, Germans, and Swiss. Sensing little interest on the part of the carabinieri, the shelter's manager telephoned the news also to the Austrian gendarmerie post in the upper Oetz Valley on the opposite side of the border. One can hear the sigh of the officer who took the call; the gendarmerie, Austria's rural police force comparable to Italy's carabinieri, has to rescue or recover scores of casualties in the mountain provinces every season. Learning that the person on the Similaun must have been dead for quite some time, the gendarmerie officer promised: "We'll investigate the case tomorrow."

♨

CORPSE NO. 619/91

Next morning, a Friday, the manager of the Similaun Refuge himself climbed to the glacier site indicated to him by the German tourists and saw the body sticking out of the ice. He had thought he would find the remains of an Alpinist who had died in an accident and was puzzled not to see any of the paraphernalia that climbers usually carry with them—no snow goggles, no ice ax, no rope. The mummylike body suggested to young Pirpamer that it must have been dead for many years.

That afternoon an Austrian gendarme landed on the Similaun in a helicopter and tried to free the trapped body with a jackhammer. In the process the garment and skin of the dead person were torn, but luckily there wasn't enough compressed air for the power tool to wreak further damage. The gendarmes in the valley said later they would get the body out of the ice as soon as the helicopter wasn't needed for more urgent missions.

Meanwhile word of the discovery on the Similaun had spread locally, and several curious people climbed up to the glacier. Among them was Reinhold Messner, a South Tyrolean freeclimber who had won fame by scaling Mount Everest and other of the world's highest peaks with minimal equipment. The hirsute Messner, who lived in the old Juval Castle near the mouth of the Schnals Valley/Val Senales, and a friend, Hans Kammerlander, said they had been on a tour of outstanding mountains on either side of the Italian-Austrian border and happened to be in the Similaun Refuge when they learned of the discovery higher up. They climbed to the glacier, and Messner took pictures of the body.

Messner, who was known to have extensive contacts with the information media, tipped off journalists that a human body, maybe hundreds of years old, had been found on the Similaun, giving many the impression that he himself had made the discovery. Local amateur historians at once came up with a theory: the dead man may have been a henchman of Frederick IV, duke of Tyrol, who during a power struggle in the early fifteenth century hid out for some time in a high-mountain farm near the Similaun (where he was supposed to have also found romance). Frederick IV, an always debt-ridden Hapsburg prince who was dubbed "Empty Pockets," died in 1439; the South Tyroleans never forgot him because he had curbed the arrogance of local barons and petty lords and had favored the common people during his sensible administration.

The circumstance of Messner's name being mentioned in connection with the find on the Similaun caused rumors that the whole matter was a prank played on the South Tyrolean record climber. Messner had once claimed he had spotted tracks of yeti, the "Abominable Snowman," in the Himalayas, and some German newspapers had made fun of him because of that episode. Now there were suggestions that a corpse had been planted in the ice as bait for the attention-seeker Messner or even that he himself had staged a false discovery.

During the more than three days between the body's sighting by the German tourist couple and its eventual recovery by Austrian police, dozens of people saw it, took pictures, touched it, and may have removed material as a souvenir. The Iceman also suffered rough treatment when he was freed from the glacier.

In the morning of Monday, September 23, a helicopter with Austrian gendarmes and an expert on forensic medicine from Innsbruck, Dr. Rainer Henn, landed on the Italian side of Mount Similaun and walked to the spot where the body had been discovered. They found that because of a drop in temperature it was again imprisoned in ice and proceeded to get it out with a pickax and ski poles. A chartered helicopter with an Austrian television crew and journalists had preceded the official party to the Similaun.

The recovery team wrapped the mummy in a plastic sheet, put it in a body bag, and loaded it with the objects found near it—including a metal ax and shreds of clothing—on their helicopter. The body was taken in a hearse from the Austrian village of Vent in the upper Oetz Valley to the Institute of Forensic Medicine in the regional capital, Innsbruck. Like any other corpse delivered to the morgue, it received a registration number: 619/91. The Innsbruck morgue appears to be a busy place.

∞

A TYROLEAN TUTANKHAMEN?

The next morning Professor Konrad Spindler, chief of Innsbruck University's Institute of Prehistory, visited the morgue, was stunned by the mummified body, the ax, and the other objects, and declared that the discovery had immense scientific importance. In the afternoon a press conference was held with the recovered body and the pieces of equipment found near it laid out on a dissecting table. Newspeople crowded around, touched the corpse, smoked, and cracked jokes. The films and pictures taken by the cameramen soon went around the world.

Meanwhile moldy patches had appeared on the body's skin and seemed to be spreading. The mummy was treated with fungicide, enveloped in a sterilized plastic sheet, and transferred to the university's nearby Anatomical Institute. There it was placed in a ten-by-twenty-foot (three-by-six-meter) refrigerated room kept permanently at minus six degrees centigrade (twenty-one degrees Fahrenheit), the presumed temperature to which the body had been exposed when it was trapped by the glacier. The air humidity was kept at 96–98 percent to simulate the Similaun environment.

Scientists in Austria and elsewhere soon voiced dismay at the inexpert handling the Iceman had suffered during five days, although they were thrilled by what had been salvaged and by additional discoveries.

On September 25, when a storm prevented another helicopter flight to the Similaun peak, Innsbruck glaciologist Professor

Gernot Patzelt and a few other experts made an ascent on foot for a new survey of the site where the body had emerged. They found a fur quiver containing fourteen arrows and delivered it to Innsbruck University. Independently, Italian carabinieri also searched the spot, recovering what were later identified as tatters from the Iceman's clothing and the remains of a mat, and handed the material to scientists in Bolzano.

In Innsbruck the objects stored at the university—but not, this time, the body—were shown to journalists and photographers in another press conference. When participants asked to see the arrows, the request was denied on the ground that the quiver had first to be x-rayed before its contents could be removed.

Initially Professor Spindler suggested that the Iceman had lived in the Bronze Age—in central Europe the period between 2000 and 750 B.C.—because he had mistakenly assumed that the ax found with the body was made of a copper-and-tin alloy. When the material was eventually analyzed as pure copper, the dating was revised to the late Stone Age (from about 10,000 B.C. to 2000 B.C.), during which some tools and weapons were manufactured with the unalloyed metal. Such Neolithic copper artifacts were found earlier in Switzerland, Croatia, and other places. Eventually radio-carbon dating of tiny particles of the Iceman's body, sent to scientific centers in Oxford, Paris, Uppsala in Sweden, and Zurich, determined the Iceman's age as between 4,800 and 5,500 years; 5,300 years appeared to be the likeliest figure.

It is not clear whether the Iceman's copper ax was made locally; it may have been obtained from traders who are believed to have roamed the Alps long before recorded history. Scientists say that copper was found as green veins in the rocks and as dark layers on stone surfaces of some Alpine areas in the late Stone

Age and that the metal may also have occasionally turned up in pure or nearly pure form as nuggets.

The ax, the only metal item discovered with the body on Mount Similaun, was surely a precious possession at that time and in that place. Actually, people in other parts of Europe were then already familiar with the metallurgy of bronze; Sumerians in the Near East were living in cities; the first pyramids were about to be built in Egypt; and the Chinese were using agricultural implements and may already have invented the culture of silk.

Professor Spindler told reporters it had been "the most exciting day in my professional life" when he first set eyes on the shriveled body of the Iceman. The British archaeologist Howard Carter, he mused, must have felt similar emotions when he opened Tutankhamen's tomb in 1922. The Leipzig-born scientist later said he regretted these remarks. In his 1993 book *Der Mann im Eis* (C. Bertelsmann, Munich) he wrote, "I didn't think of anything" on first seeing the Iceman except anticipating that he and his colleagues would have a lot of work to do.

Some Egyptian mummies—though not Pharaoh Tutankhamen's—are more than 4,000 years old. Yet the brain, intestines, and other vital organs are missing from them, having been removed in a lengthy treatment by embalmers before the emptied body shell was placed in a sarcophagus and ritually interred. The Iceman's scientific value is enhanced by his completeness: eyes, brain, heart, lungs, and stomach with its contents were conserved by the glacier as they were when he died. Relatively intact bodies found earlier in moors, peat, and salt mines in various countries were all younger than is *Homo tyrolensis*.

THE ICEMAN

WHOSE MUMMY IS IT?

News of the Similaun discovery brought such an avalanche of inquiries from all over the world that the Austrian postal administration hurriedly installed additional telephone lines at Innsbruck University. Specialists and scientific institutions in many countries offered assistance in the evaluation of the glacial find or asked for snippets of the body and equipment for analyses and tests of their own.

A commission of scientists and officials set up in Vienna by Austria's minister of science, Erhard Busek, eventually decided that the Iceman's body should remain in Innsbruck, entrusted to the university's Anatomical Institute, while his equipment should be sent to Mainz, Germany. The research and restoration center for prehistory of the Roman-German Central Museum in Mainz was the most appropriate institution for evaluating the objects found near the body, the Vienna commission stated. Scientists from many nations started the study of the Iceman's equipment in Mainz.

When it awarded the coveted research project to the Mainz center, the Austrian government all but ignored Italian claims to the Iceman. A week after the German couple had first seen the body, Italians realized that a big blunder had been committed by the carabinieri when they had advised the manager of the Similaun Refuge to ask the Austrian police to recover it. Now Italian officials and information media, alerted by the vast international echo of the discovery, contended that it had been made on their nation's territory and that the body and the equipment must be turned over to Italy. Messner, one of the first persons on the site, backed the Italian stand.

The governments of Austria and Italy agreed to have a joint commission establish with exactitude the borderline between the two states on the Similaun. A team from the Italian Institute of Military Geography in Florence was dispatched to South Tyrol to rendezvous with Austrian surveyors on the mountain. The three geographers from Florence never reached the Similaun. After arriving in Bolzano, they learned that strong squalls prohibited a trip to the peak by helicopter. They proceeded by car to the Oetz Valley on the Austrian side. There, at the village of Sölden, they found they would have to climb for hours on foot to the glacier field. The trio had arrived from Florence wearing light business suits and city shoes; they quickly called off their expedition.

Meanwhile, however, the Austrian surveyors who had been waiting vainly for their Italian colleagues, had established that the Iceman had been found 92.56 meters (303.67 feet) south of the international border, between frontier markers nos. 36 and 37—clearly on Italian territory.

The Austrians acknowledged that the gendarmes had acted improperly, though in good faith, when they recovered the body from the glacier and took it to Innsbruck. This caused satisfaction in Rome and above all in South Tyrol. Tyroleans south and north of the Brenner Pass usually see eye to eye in issues involving the Italian central government; in the dispute on whether the Iceman had been discovered on Italian or Austrian territory, the South Tyroleans nevertheless sided with Rome.

Yet when Italy's national government was considering an official request that Austria must transfer the prehistoric body and equipment to Rome, the South Tyroleans protested. The government of the autonomous province of Bolzano/Südtirol discussed the case at a special meeting and in a statement declared that the Similaun find was a historical-cultural asset that according to the laws belonged to South Tyrol and not to the Italian state.

The head of the provincial government, Luis Durnwalder, said there were no objections to having *Homo tyrolensis* examined scientifically in Innsbruck for the time being, but that the body must eventually be moved to Bozen/Bolzano. South Tyrol has no university (although it planned to create "academic structures") and no facility comparable to the Innsbruck Institutes of Forensic Medicine and Anatomy.

A week later Durnwalder met with his Austrian counterpart, the governor of the Tyrol region, Alois Partl, in a joint visit to the Iceman at Innsbruck University. "He is the ur-Tyrolean [original Tyrolean]," Partl affirmed.

In February 1992 Innsbruck University, in a formal accord with the autonomous province of Bolzano/Südtirol, undertook to return the Iceman and the objects found near the body to South Tyrol within three years. The term, it was stated, might be extended if necessary. During another meeting in Innsbruck in September 1993, two years after the Similaun discovery, the South Tyrolean government chief, Durnwalder, remarked that the Iceman might be taken to Bozen/Bolzano within two years—a year later than originally scheduled. "The mummy belongs to South Tyrol, but of course it belongs in the first place to humankind and to the scientific community, which must have time to study it," Durnwalder said. Under the agreement between Bolzano and Innsbruck, all income from publications and other sources connected with *Homo tyrolensis* was to be used for the conservation and appraisal of the finds.

South of the Brenner Pass a project was aired to build a special museum, possibly in Bolzano, for the Iceman. Scientists voiced reservations, and other critics said it would be tasteless to press the Neolithic mountain climber into the role of a sight-seeing attraction. In North Tyrol the commercial exploitation of the glacial discovery had started at once. Postcards and T-shirts reproduced photos of the 5,300-year-old "Oetzi"—a nickname derived from the Oetz Valley at the foot of Mount Similaun. Fiction writers rushed their versions of how the Iceman had lived and died into print, pop musicians celebrated him in songs, and cartoonists in various countries had their fun with him.

৵৹

FINDINGS AND PUZZLES

There were also weirder reactions. A Swiss woman asserted that from the photos in the press she had identified the body as that of her husband who twenty years earlier had disappeared during a mountain tour in Tyrol; he had surely fallen into a crevasse on the Similaun and perished. She turned to Switzerland's diplomatic service to press her claim to restitution of the dead man's body but was turned down.

Several women in various parts of the world got in touch with Innsbruck University, offering to bear the Iceman's child if his semen had been conserved in the cold during the millennia. Those would-be mothers of a Stone Age baby didn't know that parts of the Iceman's penis and scrotum were missing. One explanation was that a large portion of his sexual organs had been destroyed by bacterial or other factors in the glacier into which water must have seeped during warm spells. Later the custodians of the mummy tended to assume that the rescuers who had first tried to free the body from the ice with a jackhammer and later hacked it out with a pickax had caused the mutilation. Lesions in the left hip and other regions of the body that at first were believed to have been the work of birds or other animals were eventually found to be due to inexpert handling on Mount Similaun.

An unsettling theory was that some souvenir freak had castrated the Iceman during the first few days after the discovery. The absence of a major part of the genitalia also led to farfetched journalistic speculation that the Iceman might have been a Stone Age homosexual who was forced from his village into the icy wilderness of the high mountains.

According to the preliminary findings, the Iceman at any rate seemed to have enjoyed reasonably good health. He was between twenty-five and forty years old and five feet two inches (157 centimeters) tall; human beings in the Stone Age were generally shorter than is today's European average. His weight is believed to have been around 110 pounds (50 kilograms). He had most of his teeth, but they were considerably worn. X-raying revealed that long before his death five of his left ribs had been broken, maybe in a bad fall, but that they had healed.

The Iceman's head and body were hairless, but hundreds of curly dark hairs were found in his clothing. Since none of the recovered hairs that were assumed to have come from the Iceman's head was longer than 3.5 inches (9 centimeters), the conclusion was that he had cut his hair. On the basis of the data thus far available several artists developed composite pictures of how he may have looked; to reconstruct the face and hairstyle of *Homo tyrolensis* they used portraits of past and present rural Tyrolean types for guidance. One such attempt was published by *National Geographic* magazine (June 1993), but the Innsbruck scientists didn't like it.

Tattoos on various parts of the Iceman's body caused particular puzzlement among anthropologists. There were parallel lines on the left and right sides of the lower back, a cross with arms of equal length behind the left knee, wavy stripes on the right ankle, and other stripes in various body areas that may or may not have been tattoos. The marks were blue, presumably caused by rubbing charcoal, solved in saliva or water, into punctures made in the skin with a sharp bone. Clothing must have covered the tattoos at least in the cold of the mountains. Their meaning is any scientist's guess—tribal identification, marks of some rite of initiation into adulthood, a record of slain animals or human enemies, magic, or primitive acupuncture therapy. Most specialists had until recently assumed that tattooing had started much later than the Stone Age, possibly in Africa, Asia, or Oceania.

X-raying, CAT scans, and other tests would in due course shed more light on the Iceman's physical makeup—whether he was suffering from any organic disease, how his brain was structured, how his anatomy functioned, what his DNA endowment was, what he had eaten before his death, why his short, well-worn teeth were bluish in some spots. All those data and others that the examinations over the years will yield may not answer the prime question: What was *Homo tyrolensis* doing on Mount Similaun? Where did he come from, and where did he want to go? The first genetic analysis of the body determined, at any rate, that the Iceman was European-born, closely related to present-time Alpine people.

Two mountain saddles, both a little to the west of where the Iceman lay, permit passage without much trouble, at least in summer, from the Schnals/Senales Valley in South Tyrol to the Oetz Valley north of the Alpine crest.

The Iceman was found some 1,000 feet (a little more than 300 meters) from one of the two passages, the Hauslab Joch,

10,757 feet (3,279 meters) above sea level. It is named after a nineteenth-century Austrian military geographer, General Franz von Hauslab. To most Tyroleans the Iceman may be "Oetzi," but to scientists and the Austrian bureaucracy he is the Man from the Hauslab Joch. Italians after World War I rechristened the lofty saddle Passo di Tisa after the name of an old farmstead much below it. Today the Passo di Tisa/Hauslab Joch is officially closed because neither Austria nor Italy maintains a permanent border post there. During the warm season, nevertheless, mountaineers pass through it constantly, and cattle breeders from the Schnals/Senales Valley drive sheep to the extended pastures on the Austrian side with the consent of the landowners at Vent, the village 6,211 feet (1,893 meters) up a side valley that contributes a stream to the Oetz River.

There are a few theories surrounding the Iceman's history. One is that the Iceman was a shepherd looking for pasturages north of the Similaun when a storm sprang up; he may have lost contact with companions and the flocks, sought shelter in a natural trough in the rock, fallen asleep from exhaustion, and frozen to death. This sounds credible to the present local population; even now persons lose their lives in the Alps this way year after year.

In the case of *Homo tyrolensis*, the body may have been quickly covered with snow and ice, and the advancing glacier may have formed a chamber over a rock pan that conserved it as in a refrigeration cell for 5,300 years. Protection by a rocky hollow would explain why the slow mountain stream of ice in its crawl through the millennia didn't crush and mangle the Iceman as glaciers usually do with bodies trapped in them.

Other scenarios would have the Iceman trekking on the high mountains as a hunter or trader and dying of fatigue and cold. Professor Spindler suggested he may have been under great stress, having fled into the mountain fastness after a losing fight with a rival or enemies, only to meet his death on the glacier. Another attempted explanation was that the Iceman had been a magician or shaman who ritually climbed high mountains to meet with ghosts and perished while awaiting such an apparition. Nearly all experts agreed that the man who had died on the Similaun was an experienced mountaineer. His equipment was the proof.

A Stone Age Mountaineer's Outfit

The objects found together with the body and taken to Mainz for scientific evaluation told a lot about *Homo tyrolensis* and the culture he came from. The ax, a wedge of copper with hammered edges to prevent it from slipping, inserted in a wooden shaft and fastened to it with leather straps, is of a type known from similar finds at Remedello near Brescia, close to the Alpine foothills of northern Italy, in the nineteenth century. This may be a clue that the Iceman was trying to cross the mountain ridges from south to north and not vice versa.

The bow is a length of yew, a tree that has furnished wood for such weapons from prehistoric times to the present. One tip was broken off but was recovered from the glacier site a year after the original discovery. Since notches for the bowstring are missing, the scientists theorize that the Iceman had not yet used the weapon or had earlier lost and discarded another bow. An animal sinew that may have served as a cord was found in the quiver.

It was the deerskin quiver and its contents that above all

thrilled the experts. Markus Egg, a Tyrolean-born prehistorian at the Mainz Institute, said exultantly that the artifact was the first quiver from the late Stone Age found anywhere in the world. The fourteen arrows in it were fashioned from very straight branches of dogwood and viburnum, which grow in Tyrol as shrubs and trees. Two of the arrows had been readied for shooting, with flint heads fastened to one end and feathers glued with resin to the other. Also in the quiver were pieces of deer's antlers and sinews and a tightly coiled six-foot (two-meter) cord made of the inner bark of trees.

The Iceman was also equipped with a five-inch (thirteen-centimeter) dagger—a sharp flint blade sticking from a handle of ash wood; a number of items in a belt pocket believed to have been used for kindling fires; a small rock tool that may have been a whetstone; and a polished marble disk with tassels of twisted leather strips hanging out on either side of a central hole—probably a talisman. Shreds of birch-bark containers and traces of a wooden frame that may have been part of a wooden backpack were also found with the body. The tiny bone fragments recovered from near the mummy were identified as splinters from the upper vertebrae of an ibex whose meat may have been the Iceman's last meal.

The Neolithic mountain climber was wearing leggings of goatskin held up by straps and a belt as well as a gown of tanned animal skins, skillfully stitched together with sinews and plant fibers, around his loins. Holes in the garments had been carefully mended. Furthermore, he carried a kind of blanket formed by strands of grass and straw that must have served both as outerwear and as a rudimentary sleeping bag. His much-repaired heelless shoes were of calfskin stuffed with grass for keeping warm. When the Iceman's body was recovered, the remains of one shoe, showing the wear and tear of mountain trekking, and large tufts of grass were still dangling from the right foot. A patch of fur found on the glacier site later may have been part of a conical cap blown off his head by a gust of wind.

About one hundred fragments of the Iceman's clothing, some of them minuscule, were assembled at the Roman-German Central Museum in Mainz for thorough examination. The material should provide elements for understanding the late Stone Age's environment, society, and technology. Which animals supplied the leather? How was it tanned? Do the garments show some degree of craftsmanship, suggesting that they were made by an artisan? Which trees and other plants furnished wood and vegetable parts of the Iceman's equipment, and where did they grow? These are some of the questions to be answered.

To prehistorians and anthropologists, an exciting aspect of *Homo tyrolensis* is that he was not discovered in a grave or tomb, maybe surrounded by funerary objects, but emerged from the glacier the way he was surprised by death in vigorous pursuit of some task, with the equipment he must have thought adequate to it.

The Iceman holds a special meaning for the mountaineers of the region where he was found. They hardly needed further proof that human beings climbed to the passes, ridges, glaciers, and summits of the Alps in prehistoric times; many earlier archaeological finds are evidence enough. But the Tyroleans can and do identify with the man who died a lonely death on Mount Similaun: they know the lure and hazards of the lofty pinnacles, and they have heard of, or even remember, shepherds who challenged the heights in outfits not much dissimilar from the Iceman's and succeeded or succumbed.

LUMINOUS
DOUBLE CITY

Bizarre stone formations like the teeth of a giant saw or the spires of a Gaudíesque rock cathedral are visible from the railroad station of Bolzano/Bozen and from many other points in the capital of South Tyrol. The fractured chain 12 miles (19 kilometers) southeast of the city, rising to an altitude of 9,780 feet (2,981 meters), is among the most fantastic sights of the Dolomites. Gray during daytime, the forbidding towers turn pink and purple in the setting sun—a free early-evening show in Bolzano whenever the sky is clear.

To the Tyroleans, the enormous prongs are the mythical Rosengarten, or Rose Garden. More prosaically, Italians call them the Catinaccio, or Big Chain. Through the centuries people stayed away from the wastes and screes of the Rose Garden. Two Britons ascended its highest peak in 1874; only experienced Alpinists should attempt to scale the rock spires.

Medieval legend has it that the Rose Garden was once the realm of Laurin, the king of a people of ore-mining dwarfs, a midget wizard whose magic belt gave him the strength of twelve men and whose magic cap made him invisible. He resided in a crystal underground palace. Hankering for female companionship, he donned his cap, made a foray into the lowlands, and under the cloak of invisibility during a tourney abducted Similde, daughter of the king of the Etsch (the Adige River), who was attending the knightly sport and as its prize was supposed to become the wife of the winner.

The discomfited knights asked a contemporary hero, Dietrich of Bern, to help them free the princess from the thrall of Laurin, whose army of thousands of gnomes would be prepared to defend him to the death. Dietrich, in Germanic legend, is an idealized Theoderic the Great, king of the Ostrogoths from A.D. 474 to 526. "Bern" doesn't refer to the Swiss city of that name, but to Verona, one of Theoderic's residences in northern Italy.

The Gothic hero consented and with a retinue of knights invaded Laurin's mountain domains. They marveled at the splendor of a rose garden in the midst of boulders and rocky debris, which indicated to them the entrance to the dwarf king's subterranean palace. In single combat Dietrich managed to deprive the invisible adversary of his magic belt and cap and to subdue him. Similde, accompanied by dwarf ladies-in-waiting, emerged from the mountain and pleaded for her captor's life, affirming that she had been treated well and honorably. Dietrich conducted Laurin as a prisoner to Bern (Verona), where the gnome king was to eke out a miserable living as a juggler and mountebank. He would never again see his mountains. When he was led away from his realm he uttered a curse: Nobody should ever admire his roses again, neither during the day nor at night! Laurin forgot mentioning dusk, and that's why the rocky roses light up at sunset.

The myth of Laurin and his reign of gnomes has many variations, and the theme of dwarfs recurs in many other Tyrolean folk tales, which tell of buried treasures, giants, and forest monsters. The pervasive motif of diminutive mountain dwellers in popular legend represents an important clue for prehistorians.

They interpret it as evidence that a race of short, fine-boned people lived once in this section of the Alps and mined the mountains for gold, silver, copper, and other metals.

This people of small diggers is generally identified as a northern tribe of the Illyrians, prehistoric Indo-Europeans who during the Bronze Age occupied large areas between the Danube and the Adriatic Sea. When the ancient Romans pushed northward, they found Illyrians mingled with earlier Celtic invaders, and they called the inhabitants of the country at the head of the Adriatic the Veneti. The highly civilized tribe gave its Roman name to Venice, the city founded on the islands in its lagoon in the early Middle Ages as a refuge from barbarian raiders. The root *ven* is contained also in various place names in the Alps, like Gross-Venediger, the 12,054-foot (3,674-meter) peak that marks the frontier between eastern Tyrol and the Salzburg region, and the village of Vent, near which the 5,300-year-old Iceman was discovered.

To the strapping warriors of the Germanic tribes that invaded the Tyrolean valleys in the early Middle Ages, the local population must have appeared as "dwarfs" and their mining technology and other skills seemed magical. While today's descendants of the Teutonic conquerors and settlers are blond and tall, many South Tyrolean families also include dark-haired, short persons, their bloodlines probably going back to the Veneti and to the Illyrian-Celtic mixed race that the ancient Romans called Rhaetians.

The name *Laurin* is probably one of pre-Roman and pre-Germanic origin. In the Rose Garden complex there are a Laurin's Wall, 9,229 rocky feet (2,813 meters) high, and an 8,760-foot (2,670-meter) Laurin's Pass between two rock towers. In a hollow below that pass, facing Laurin's Wall, is the so-called Gartl (Little Garden), with boulders, debris, and a small, icy lake. It is here that folk myth locates the entrance to the gnome king's crystal palace and the scene of his losing combat with Dietrich of Bern. The Little Garden is a place of great desolation.

The king of the legendary dwarf people is recalled in Bolzano by a Via Laurin/Laurin Strasse, a Laurin Hotel, a Laurin Fountain, and various other commercial and cultural references. During many hours before the evening glow of the Rose Garden, the city is filled with sunshine. An artist from North Carolina who has her studio on top of a modern building on Bolzano's northern outskirts told me: "When the weather is fair, as it often is here also in winter, the quality of the light itself urges me to paint." In summer it often gets very hot in the South Tyrolean capital, and many residents flee to second homes, to relatives, or to boardinghouses in the mountains all around.

℘

SOUTHERN IMAGE

Bolzano/Bozen, at 870 feet (265 meters) above sea level, lies in a broad basin—which in summer may become a cauldron—where the Isarco/Eisack River receives the waters of the Talvera/Talfer and about 3 miles (5 kilometers) downstream joins the Adige/Etsch in its wide valley. Northeast of Bolzano is the high plateau of the Ritten/Renon, with Oberbozen/Soprabolzano and other airy villages; toward the west the city looks out on a long, forested ridge of porphyry rock, the Mendel/Mendola.

My first experience of Bolzano was two years before World War II, when I had there a rendezvous with Maria, then my fiancée. It was late summer, and day after day the thermometer in what at the time was the Piazza Vittorio Emanuele (it is now again Piazza Walther/Waltherplatz) approached 40 degrees centigrade (104 degrees Fahrenheit). The square and the streets around it were deserted at siesta time. The city came to life only in the late afternoon, when the Rose Garden started turning pink. Italian officers in smart whites and soldiers wearing the shapeless gray-green uniforms in which Mussolini's army clad its conscripts milled around the large piazza and along the tree-lined street leading from it to the railroad station. Girls in pairs or groups promenaded up and down, feigning not to notice the ardent glances from the presumed defenders of the Fascist fatherland. Patrols made up of a sergeant and two flanking corporals stalked around the city center to make sure the military personnel would not cause or get into any trouble.

To me it seemed a thoroughly southern scene. In those days I ate a lot of luscious grapes from the Adige Valley, drank plenty of the local red wine, and tried my Italian, in which I had already reached some proficiency, on anybody who would listen to me. The principal South Tyrolean center, then counting not quite fifty thousand residents, made on me the impression of an Italian provincial city. The palm trees, magnolias, and other Mediterranean vegetation reinforced that feeling.

From the end of World War I, and especially after the Fascists had come to power in 1922, the governments in Rome had indeed made every effort to Italianize the capital of the newly acquired Alpine province. In 1921 Bolzano had about twenty-five thousand inhabitants, some seven thousand of them Italians. When I first stayed there, in 1937, the proportion of the Italian-speaking population to the German-speaking residents may have been half and half, although no statistics were available. Today

Bolzano is a city of one hundred thousand, and the mother tongue of three-quarters of them is Italian.

Under Mussolini large state-controlled and private industrial concerns built plants on Bolzano's outskirts and recruited workers from more southerly parts of the nation. The Eisack River was harnessed in a power plant upstream to provide more electricity. The army and the Fascist bureaucracy too brought much Italian personnel to the city.

Italian Bolzano lies mainly west of the Talvera River in a sheltered plain where once the separate village and winter resort of Gries was embraced by gardens and vineyards. If you were led blindfolded into the district today, you would think when the bandage was taken off that you are in a pleasant middle-class neighborhood of, say, Treviso or Varese. The streets are in a geometrical pattern, bordered by modern, flat-roofed residential buildings, many of them in the unimaginative architecture once known in Italy as *stile novecento* (twentieth-century style); the massive Palace of Justice (the courthouse) and other public edifices are pretentiously Mussolini-modern. So is the showy Church of Christ the King in red porphyry on Via Roma. As on the newer outskirts of Treviso or Varese, there are the espresso bars, supermarkets, bank branches, and shoe stores to which Italians are accustomed. Farther out, near the Bolzano South exit of the motorway and along the railroad tracks, spread motor works and other manufacturing plants, trucking enterprises, and service stations.

What has remained of old Gries is worth a visit, especially the Gothic parish church on the northwestern rim of the predominantly Italian district at the foot of Mount Guntschna/Guncinà. The edifice, surrounded by a cemetery, dates back to the twelfth century, and a side chapel on its right contains a carved altarpiece with life-size figures representing the Virgin being crowned. The expressive faces of the figures and the intricate folds of their garments are remarkable. The work, from which the wing parts are missing, was executed between 1471 and 1475 by Michael Pacher of Bruneck/Brunico, one of the most important wood-carvers and painters of the era. His famous masterpiece is the high altar in the parish church of St. Wolfgang, Austria (1481); he died in nearby Salzburg in 1498. Fifteen tempera paintings at the back of the Gries altarpiece, showing episodes of the life of Jesus and Mary, are probably by an artist from southern Germany, possibly Konrad Waider, executed around 1480.

The principal access to Italian Bolzano is from the Old Town over the Talvera/Talfer Bridge. On the river's west bank rises a structure that angers the Tyroleans as do few other things. It is the Victory Monument, which Mussolini had erected in 1928, a triumphant arch with six crenellated white marble columns. The sculptured bundles of rods around an ax with the blade sticking out—the fasces—have long been chiseled off because this emblem of fascism was banned in Italy after World War II, but their outlines are still clearly visible.

The massive monument carries a winged nude figure that may impersonate either Italy or Victory between two busts in relief with steel helmets of the shape that Italian soldiers wore in 1915–18. On the arch's side facing the Old Town a Latin inscription reads:

> *Hic Patriae Fines Siste Signa*
> *Hinc Ceteros Excoluimus Lingua Legibus Artibus.*
> *(Here establish the fatherland's boundaries*
> *From here we civilized the others through language, laws,*
> *and skills.)*

The monument with its message of ancient Roman colonialism is at present an embarrassment to many Italians. Neo-Fascist sentiment, which is strong among the Italians of Bolzano as every election shows, has so far prevented the removal of the inscription in the same way as the fasces were removed. The entire large Victory Monument is today surrounded by a steel palisade to protect it from possible outrage.

The Roman soldiers who first advanced into the Tyrolean valleys and crossed the mountain passes in 15 B.C., and then garrisoned regional centers for hundreds of years, undoubtedly brought with them their language and skills and enforced Roman law. "The others," namely the local population who were thus colonized and, at least superficially, Latinized, were Veneti and Illyrian-Celtic Rhaetians. The Germanic invaders came and settled later during the decline and fall of the Roman Empire, and they imported their own language and customs with them but were in turn influenced by the cultural environment they found— the Christian religion, viticulture, and the copper and silver mines worked by the "gnomes."

જાજી

TYROLEAN CORE

The original Bozen, east of the Talvera/Talfer River, has a Tyrolean core with arcaded burghers' houses from the seventeenth century and a colorful, lively market. In newer neighborhoods buildings in *Jugendstil* (youth style)—the central European version of the flowery turn-of-the-century art nouveau—stand side by side with official and private structures erected during the Fascist regime and with modern housing. The Tyrolean dialect prevails in the market, but many Italian speakers too live in the older districts or work in jobs there; the city is bilingual.

Visitors arriving by car or train gravitate toward Waltherplatz/ Piazza Walther, as I did when it was Piazza Vittorio Emanuele. The large, rectangular square is enclosed by modern buildings and lined with hotels, restaurants, espresso bars, and stores catering to tourists. Bolzano's young generation of Italians favors the Mc-Donald's franchise in the piazza's northwest, while transiting German tourists spoon gelato at the outdoor tables of the local cafes, and local people occupying the few public benches chat or read newspapers.

At the center of the square rises the much photographed monument to Walther von der Vogelweide, the greatest of the lyrical poets in the German language in the Middle Ages. South Tyroleans are convinced that Walther—who lived between about 1170 and 1230, generations before Dante and Chaucer—was one of them. The village of Waidbruck/Ponte Gardena, 16 miles (25 kilometers) northeast of Bolzano, is one of several places claiming to have brought forth Walther. An ancient farmhouse on a nearby hill belonging to the village of Lajen (page 162) is known as the Vogelweid Hof and carries a memorial plaque; the family that has owned it for the last few centuries keeps a visitors' book.

Vogelweide means an area where birds feed, an unofficial bird sanctuary, and as a part of the poet's name the word is interpreted as an indication that he belonged to the lesser Tyrolean nobility. When I first stayed in Sterzing/Vipiteno, I was shown a nearby forested patch and told it was called the Upper and Lower Vogelweide and that Walther had surely hailed from some nearby place.

Little is known about the poet's life; modern research has

found reasons for conjecturing that instead of in Tyrol he may have been born in lower Austria, maybe in the surroundings of Vienna, or somewhere in southern Germany. He himself said in a poem that in Vienna he had learned to "sing and tell"—the art of minstrelsy. He was attached to the lively court of Duke Friedrich I in Vienna between 1190 and 1198 and after his generous patron's death wandered from court to princely court in the way of a troubadour. He may have spoken the French or the Provençal language and almost certainly was acquainted with the Romance poetry of southern France. Walther must have composed his own music to his verses, but it has been lost.

In one moving poem he tells that after a life in foreign parts he had returned to his native country. Was it South Tyrol? He doesn't say. It might have been, but there is no conclusive evidence. "Alas, where have all my years gone?" Walther sighs. "Has my life been a dream? I don't recognize what once was as familiar to me as my own hand. The people and the land where I grew up have become strange, and my former playmates old and tired. The fields are wasted and the trees have been cut down. If the waters didn't flow as they used to do, I should be desperate." The stream or river may or may not have been the upper Eisack.

Walther revisited Vienna in 1217; in his poetry he proclaimed himself a partisan of contemporary political movements; urged the German princes to go on a Crusade against the infidel; and kept celebrating true love. He is said to have died in Würzburg, Bavaria, and to have been buried there. According to tradition, he willed that the birds be fed on his grave every day.

More often than not, when I saw the Walther Monument in Bolzano a pigeon or blackbird was perched on the statue's head. The minnesinger (love singer) was sculpted in white marble from the upper Etsch/Adige Valley by Heinrich Natter in 1889 as a still youthful man with long hair flowing from his cap, wrapped in a cape and holding a lute. Water gushes from the beak of a swan at the foot of the statue, and two lions on either side hold Tyrolean coats of arms.

The Fascist authorities, resenting the testimonial to medieval Germanic literature in Bolzano's main square, removed it in 1935 from what was then Piazza Vittorio Emanuele to an inconspicuous park. In 1981 the Walther Monument returned to the space that was again, this time in two languages, called Walther Square. A three-level parking garage is now invisibly below it.

The northwestern corner of Walther Square is taken up by the choir of what used to be the Old Town's parish church and is now the cathedral of the diocese's bishop. After residing for more than a thousand years in or near the "Tyrolean Rome," the city of Brixen/Bressanone, the religious leaders of the Roman Catholics in the province of Bolzano/Südtirol have had their episcopal see in its capital since 1964.

The Gothic church is more than six hundred years old. Its roof is covered with colored, glazed tiles; the elegant belfry, 213 feet (70 meters) tall, with a lacework stone spire, was rebuilt after a fire in 1499. The church again suffered heavy damage by Allied bombing during World War II but was quickly repaired afterward. When entering the cathedral, note the two red marble lions flanking the Lombard-style portal on the west side. In the imposing interior with three naves the sculpted, late-Gothic pulpit and a Baroque marble altar stand out. Services in the cathedral are held in Italian and German. The bishops of Bozen and Brixen/ Bolzano and Bressanone who succeeded each other in recent years were Tyroleans and stressed interethnic concord. Occasionally, concerts of sacred music are held in their cathedral for a bilingual audience.

❦

MERCANTILE SPIRIT

From the north side of Waltherplatz a lane leads to Kornmarkt (Grain Market), Bolzano's oldest square, and to Laubengasse/Via dei Portici, its principal shopping street and a pedestrian mall. Local people and tourists jostle one another under the arcades of the narrow old houses with gray, pink, or green facades and bow windows.

The most important edifice in the street, on its south side, is the Mercantile Building, erected in the early eighteenth century as a kind of business arbitration board and Chamber of Commerce. It is a handsome Italianate palazzo with outdoor stairs and a double portal at its main facade, which is on Silbergasse or Via Argentieri (Silversmith Street). Today concerts, recitals, and, occasionally, art auctions are held in the building's large hall.

The stores and boutiques on Laubengasse display Italian fashions, products of genuine or make-believe Tyrolean handicrafts, leatherware, and above all shoes of every description, from dainty, high-heeled numbers for women and supple designer moccasins for men to heavy-duty mountaineers' footwear and high-tech running shoes and ski boots. The Athesia Bookstore at 41 Laubengasse offers a vast assortment of literature on the region, "Tyrolensia," some of it also in English.

At the west end of the Laubengasse is the large, oval Obstmarkt (Fruit Market) or Piazza delle Erbe, whose stands compose a palette of seasonal colors; cherries, strawberries, apricots, peaches,

64

pears, plums, apples, grapes, and vegetables are grown in the nearby fertile valleys and on the terraced slopes as well as oranges, eggplants, artichokes, and other produce from the south.

Bolzano's vocation as a trade center, as showcased today by the Laubengasse stores and Fruit Market stands, struck Goethe when he passed through the town at the start of his Italian journey in 1787. "I was glad to see the faces of so many merchants at once," he wrote. "They had an air of purpose and wellbeing." Goethe also noted the lively commerce in fruits and silk at the Bolzano market and reported that traders were bringing to it all the leather they could procure in the Tyrolean mountains. Instead, Mozart father and son, who stopped over fifteen years earlier, hadn't cared for Bolzano. "A pig's hole," the sixteen-year-old Wolfgang Amadeus wrote home, and his father, Leopold, found the town "sad."

Bolzano/Bozen has at any rate been a marketplace of regional importance since the High Middle Ages; its mercantile role intensified during the nineteenth century, when it became a railroad hub. The trains of the Brenner route and the network of highways bring hundreds of thousands of visitors or transients to the city every year. The Brenner Motorway skirts Bolzano on its east, passing above its industrial district on a long viaduct. Quite a few long-distance travelers get off Autostrada A-22, the motorway, at the northern or southern exit to spend a few hours in the city to window-shop or pick up some souvenir and get at least an ice-cream cone in Walther Square. They too help keep Bolzano prosperous.

Visitors who have a little more time and would like to get the feel of the region should set aside an hour for the Civic Museum, distant from the Fruit Market by only a five-minute walk. Take the Museumsstrasse, turning left before the Talvera/

Talfer Bridge, which leads to the Victory Monument and Italian Bolzano.

The ground floor of the museum at 14 Sparkassen-Strasse contains funerary objects, tools, ornaments, and other finds from the Bronze and Iron Ages; a decorated bronze belt and a few other rare Rhaetian items; and ancient Roman material. The upper floors are filled with reconstructions of farmhouses and burghers' rooms with authentic furniture; a collection of folk costumes from the early nineteenth century; ancient paintings and sculptures; carnival masks; and many samples of work by South Tyrolean artisans.

Two medieval convents with quiet cloisters are also noteworthy. One is adjacent to the Franciscan Church, 5 Franziskaner-Gasse, off the Fruit Market. The late-Romanesque arcaded passage dates from the fourteenth century; traces of a Crucifixion fresco are visible. The friars grow Alpine and Mediterranean flowers and plants in the courtyard. The Franciscan Church, badly damaged by bombs in 1944, has been restored, and its beautiful late-Gothic carved altar in the choir is intact. A part of the convent is at present being used for symposiums and business meetings.

The Dominican Church and convent at Kapuzinergasse, west of the cathedral, are remarkable for frescoes of biblical scenes from the fourteenth and fifteenth centuries in the St. John's Chapel that betray the influence of Giotto; unfortunately, large patches are damaged. The cloister too shows traces of late-medieval frescoes. Much of the Dominican Convent is today taken up by the Claudio Monteverdi Music Conservatory. A prestigious international piano competition, named after the virtuoso and composer Ferruccio Busoni (1866–1924), is held in late summer every year in the institution's concert hall.

The five-towered Maretsch/Mareccio Castle, adjoining vineyards on the city's northern outskirts, close to the promenade along the left (east) bank of the Talvera/Talfer River, was first erected in the thirteenth century and repeatedly rebuilt. It is today a convention center. The river promenade with its broad lawns and stunning vistas of the Rose Garden to the east provides the citizenry, especially young people, with plenty of space for walking, jogging, and playing. Keep away from it after dark, however; Bolzano has a narcotics scene, and the river shores are among the areas where druggies meet dealers.

ↄↄ

SPLIT PERSONALITY

The carabinieri and the state police include Tyroleans who speak Italian and German; the two rivaling law enforcement bodies represent the central government in Rome. So do the prefect of the province, the administrative apparatus headed by him, the law courts, the tax office, and the large army establishment. The autonomous province of Bolzano/Südtirol too has built a vast bureaucratic machine. Thus thousands of Bolzano residents are paid by the central, regional, provincial, or municipal governments. Italians are dominant in the state offices, the judiciary, and the uniformed forces. Tyroleans, instead, prevail in the provincial administration. Economic power in Bolzano is mainly in the hands of old-established Tyrolean families who own many stores, hotels, and other local businesses, wield influence in the banks and cooperatives, and have connections throughout the province.

It is a complicated system, but it has achieved a sort of ethnic-political equilibrium and widespread prosperity. A few words are in order here to retrace how the present situation developed.

When Hitler annexed Austria in 1938, the Italians were shocked to find soldiers of his Third Reich stationed at the Brenner Pass frontier. Remembrances of foreign invasions from the north are in Italian bones, and fears were then general that Nazi expansionism might soon be tempted to claim also South Tyrol in the same way as Hitler just then was claiming the Sudeten region of Czechoslovakia.

To allay Italian worries and to harden the Berlin-Rome Axis, Hitler proposed a deal to Mussolini, and it was perfected in June 1939: The German-speaking residents of the province of Bolzano and of a few adjacent areas in the neighboring provinces must choose between Italian or German citizenship; anyone deciding to remain under Italian sovereignty would have to conform with the nation's laws to the letter; those who preferred to become Germans must emigrate to the Reich.

The dilemma with which the South Tyroleans were confronted was called the Option. It caused anguish to many people, lacerated friendships and family ties, and brought about an upheaval in the Alpine society. Peasants whose ancestors had for generations lived in the same mountain farmhouse were most reluctant to leave; young people from landless families were the first to sign up for a German passport. Nazi activists brought considerable pressure on the general population to abandon their region. The Option was presented as a chance to demonstrate against Italy.

More than 80 percent of those eligible opted for emigration to greater Germany. The minority who preferred to remain in their native environment were called *Dableiber*, or stayers-on, and were reviled by the Nazi sympathizers. My fiancée and her mother, brother, and sister, though not property owners, all chose not to take part in the proposed exodus. By then I had myself become an emigré, having moved from Vienna to Rome after the Nazi takeover of Austria, and made a living, first as a hotel receptionist and then as a foreign correspondent.

The Option process in South Tyrol coincided with the start of World War II and as a consequence of it soon slowed down. During the following years the candidates for resettlement in Hitler's domains received contradictory promises: land in Burgundy in northeastern France would be assigned to them; no, they would go to Luxembourg; no, they would get new homes and plenty of fertile land in the Crimea! Some eighty thousand South Tyroleans actually left and were provisionally sent to places in Austria, Bavaria, and the areas severed from Czechoslovakia.

After the collapse of the Fascist regime in July 1943 and Italy's armistice with the Allied powers in September of that year, the German army occupied South Tyrol, and many former inhabitants who had emigrated drifted back. Thousands of younger ones didn't—they had died in Hitler's war.

When Austria's independence was restored after World War II, the government in Vienna requested that the population of South Tyrol be given an opportunity for self-determination in a plebiscite about their region's future status. The Allies rejected the demand. In 1946 Austria and Italy reached in Paris an agreement calling for special measures to safeguard the ethnic character and promote the cultural and economic development of the German-speaking population group in Bolzano Province. Since then the South Tyroleans have won a considerable autonomy in many fields, as shown in chapter 1.

In Bolzano/Bozen, as in the other centers of the province, the bilingual and bicultural system produces curious results. There is a Goethe-Strasse and a Via Dante; in the outlying neighborhoods where new street names have to be devised, zoning commissions trade their national glories: You want a Walther-von-der-Vogelweide-Strasse? We must get a Piazza Petrarca! You insist on a Piazza Verdi? We need a Mozart-Allee! In Bolzano/Bozen and in the other cities and towns of the province, the streets are a *Who's Who* of two cultural pantheons.

જી

ENVIABLE ENVIRONS

The Ritten/Renon, a vast, hilly plateau more than 1,000 feet (300–350 meters) above Bolzano, has a better climate than the South Tyrolean capital. In summer the temperature in the resort villages on the green highlands is distinctly lower and the air much purer than they are in the sweltering city; in winter, when the Ritten/Renon is free from the fog that invades the valleys, it enjoys more sunshine and often is warmer than Bolzano. The panorama of the Rose Garden and other Dolomite walls and pinnacles is grandiose.

One curious sight on the Ritten—for instance, in the valley of the Finsterbach (Dark Stream) near the village of Klobenstein/Collalbo—are pillarlike earth formations, up to nearly 100 feet (30 meters) tall and close together, some with granite or porphyry stones on top (the "Crowned Girls"). They are the remains of an Ice Age moraine; their bizarre shapes are caused by rainwater eroding material around glacial boulders and debris, mixed with loam. Sometimes the "Girls" collapse and new ones rise nearby; they seem to wander.

In a few areas of the high plateau stretches of an ancient road, paved with flagstones, can be seen. It was probably built by the ancient Romans; what is sure is that in the Middle Ages the

German emperors rode on this route across the Ritten toward the Etsch/Adige Valley. A road across the gorges of the lower Eisack River through which the Brenner Highway, Brenner railroad, and Brenner Motorway A-22 now run, was opened only in the fourteenth century and was initially practicable only for walkers, mules, and horsemen, but not for vehicles.

Until 1965 a narrow-gauge railway with rack-and-pinion stretches climbed the Ritten/Renon from a point northeast of Walther Square. Now an aerial cableway to the high plateau departs from there, sweeping over terraced vineyards and cliffs. Nostalgic rail buffs get out of the gondola at the Maria Himmelfahrt/Assunta stop to board an antique coach of what has remained of the old Ritten railway—a 4.3-mile (7-kilometer) section with stops at Oberbozen/Soprabolzano, altitude 4,003 feet (1,220 meters), and other villages and hamlets. The small stations have been restored in the style of 1907, the year when the line was opened. The Ritten railway ends at Klobenstein/Collalbo, which is 3,904 feet (1,190 meters) above sea level and affords magnificent vistas. Sigmund Freud and the women of the Freud family were repeatedly guests at the still existing Bemelmans Post Hotel, 8 Dorfstrasse, and used to take long walks.

The plateau can be reached also by car over a highway, opened in 1965, branching off the Via Renon/Ritten-Strasse on Bolzano's northeastern outskirts. Environmentalists say the road should never have been built because it resulted in an invasion of the heights by motor traffic. Determined hikers climb the Ritten/Renon from Bolzano on various footpaths that start in the city's northeast; the ascent takes two hours or so. The gently rolling highlands with their fields, vineyards, gardens, wooded patches, and little lakes are a permanent invitation to leisurely strolls.

The northern part of the Ritten/Renon is also an area for cross-country and downhill skiing. Ski lifts connect with the pistes on the Schwarzsee-Spitze, altitude 6,791 feet (2,070 meters), and the 7,418-foot (2,260-meter) Rittnerhorn, respectively 5 and 6.5 miles (about 8 and 10 kilometers) north of Klobenstein/Collalbo. Many of the more than seventy hotels and pensions on the high plateau are open most of the year.

Various other hills and mountains around Bolzano also command fine views and attract excursionists all year round. The Virgl/Virgolo rises as a steep rock above the east bank of the Eisack River; a panoramic terrace is at 1,499 feet (457 meters) altitude. It takes thirty to forty-five minutes to climb the hill, and various taverns offer rest and relaxation to hikers. Ruins of a medieval castle, a frescoed medieval Chapel of St. Vigil (which has given the rock its name), and a Baroque three-hundred-year-old Church of the Calvary are also there. Deep underneath incessant north-south traffic rumbles through the long Virgl Tunnel of the A-22 Motorway.

Mount Guntschna/Guncinà northwest of Bolzano is ascended on a winding promenade across vineyards that starts near the old Gries parish church. When the neighborhoods on the west bank of the Talvera/Talfer River were a separate village and health resort where one would spend the winter and spring months, resident doctors advised their patients to amble up the Guntschna promenade or at least part of it to test themselves and do some deep breathing. At about 1,600 feet (500 meters) altitude and a little higher there are various cafes and pleasant footpaths. The vistas of Bolzano and of the Rose Garden to the east are superb.

To me the most gratifying side trip from Bolzano is up the Sarntal/Val Sarentina to the north. It is a narrow valley, deeply

cut into the mountains by the Talvera/Talfer River; gorges enclosed by red porphyry walls alternate with wider stretches where
isolated farmhouses, wooden barns, and the occasional chapel
stand below dark forests. After a sequence of tunnels the traveler
reaches some hamlet or village. Tumbling rocks, landslides, and
avalanches often cut the road, National Route 508, and the river
may spill over its banks after heavy rains and sweep away some
bridge. There are three dozen hotels and inns in the approximately
30-mile (50-kilometer) valley, but the Sarntal/Val Sarentina is
much less touristy than many other areas in the province.

The old folkways are lingering especially in a lonely side
valley, Durnholzer Tal/Val Durna, with a little lake high up. At
Reinwald/San Martino at the head of that side valley the village
priest still takes in paying guests in his whitewashed, tiny parish
house, a custom once widespread in the region. The folk costumes
in the Sarntal/Val Sarentina are renowned for their authenticity.

Entering the valley from Bolzano by car or public bus, after
little more than 1 mile (2 kilometers), the first-time visitor will
gasp at the thirteenth-century Runkelstein/Roncolo Castle, an
aerie forbiddingly sitting on top of a high, craggy porphyry rock
at 1,381 feet (421 meters) altitude. It belongs today to the city
of Bolzano and can be toured. It is remarkable above all for
frescoes from the fourteenth to the sixteenth centuries representing mythological, classical, and medieval personages like Hector,
Caesar, Charlemagne, Tristan and Iseult, and German emperors
as well as scenes from chivalrous and court life, knights at a
tournament, and rural labors with peasants, woodcutters, and farm
animals. The murals were repeatedly restored. An inscription in
archaic German above the alcove of a bow window reads "Love
Brings Sorrow." Refreshments can be had in the castle's courtyard
or, in the cold months, in a cozy room with a tiled stove.

The main town of the valley, Sarntheim/Sarentino, is some 12 miles (19 kilometers) north of Bolzano, 3,169 feet (966 meters) above sea level in a lovely position with extensive forests and two old castles in its vicinity. The little Gothic church of St. Cyprian in the middle of Sarntheim, opposite the five-hundred-year-old Inn at the Sign of the Stag, is decorated with frescoes, which have been freshened, picturing episodes from the legendary life of its patron saint.

National Route 508 proceeds past various hamlets to the Pennser Joch/Passo Pennes at an altitude of 7,267 feet (1,910 meters) near the headwaters of the Talvera/Talfer. For another 10 miles (16 kilometers) across a rather somber mountainscape, the highway descends to Ridnaun/Ridanna, a skiing center near Sterzing/Vipiteno.

IV.

HEART
OF TYROL

∾

From Bolzano it takes only little more than half an hour by
train to reach the province's second city, Merano/Meran. By
bus or car the travel time may be longer because the traffic on
National Route 38 is usually very heavy; the 18 miles (29 kilometers) of highway between the two South Tyrolean centers are
often congested like a big city's downtown street during peak
hours. A new superhighway between the two cities, long opposed by environmentalists, was not yet completed at the time
of writing.

The Etsch/Adige Valley is two miles (more than three kilometers) wide all the way between Bolzano and Merano. The
river is channeled between flood-control walls while a system of
narrow canals waters the plains on either bank—a green carpet
of vineyards and fruit plantations. Agribusiness has standardized
production; it's a Tyrolean Napa Valley. Apples, for instance,
which once were grown locally in many varieties, seem now to
be produced only in two marketable types, Delicious and Golden.

The traveler catches glimpses of ruined castles on the heights.
One of them, on a reddish porphyry spur in the northeast, is
Greifenstein (Griffin Stone), also known as the "Pig's Castle," a
few miles outside Bolzano. It seems that during a siege in the

early fifteenth century the stronghold's defenders threw a pig over the walls as defiant proof that they had plenty to eat; they nevertheless had to surrender two years later.

Merano and its famously charming environs are the very heart of South Tyrol. The nearby Tirol Castle has indeed furnished the name for the entire region both south and north of the Brenner Pass, from the Trentino to the Bavarian Alps and from the Swiss Canton Graubünden (Grisons) to Carinthia. During the Middle Ages Merano was for some time the capital of all of Tyrol.

Today Merano is an elegant resort whose balmy climate, lush vegetation, and comfortable hotels attract an international— especially German—clientele all year around; spring and autumn are its best seasons. The city is also a convenient base for trips into the Vinschgau/Val Venosta, where many place names recall the pre-Roman Rhaetian population. Medieval hilltop castles glower down on the broad, sunny Etsch/Adige Valley and its friendly old towns. Another possible side trip is into the Passeier Valley/Val Passiria, which is green in its lower reaches and wild higher up; it treasures memories of the heroic period of the Tyroleans' rebellion against Napoleon.

Merano, with 35,000 permanent residents, counts more than 150 hotels and pensions, some of them luxurious, with nearly 10,000 beds. The city, 1,063 feet (324 meters) above sea level, is sheltered by soaring mountains to its north and abounds in parks and private gardens; the luxuriant vegetation of tall palms, almond and laurel trees, oleander, jasmine, and other Mediterranean plants contributes to the Riviera ambiance. Flower beds in dazzling colors line the promenades along the Passer/Passirio torrent, which separates the city center on its right (north) bank from the newer, chic districts of Obermais and Untermais (Italian:

Maia Alta and Maia Bassa). The torrent joins the Etsch/Adige south of the city.

As a spa, Merano has claimed since the early nineteenth century that the waters from about one hundred springs in the adjacent hillside possess special therapeutic properties. As physical and medical insights and fashions changed, the cause of these presumed benign characteristics were variously described. Once Merano vaunted the radioactivity of its waters and climate; at present the spa literature speaks of the area's two principal "radon medical springs." Radon, a radioactive gaseous element, is defined as a "noble gas" that remains only a short time in the human body and, in the words of a Merano promotional pamphlet, "volatilizes without any harmful influence in a few hours after setting off biological reactions on which its therapeutic effect is based."

The waters of Merano are said to produce favorable results in the treatment of rheumatic and arthritic ailments, pulmonary and respiratory diseases, gynecological and urinary problems, arteriosclerosis, and old-age complaints. The vast Municipal Spa Center on the left (south) bank of the Passer and the health sections of some hotels offer facilities for bathing and water-drinking procedures, massages, inhalations, and mud-pack applications.

The Municipal Spa Center comprises large outdoor and covered swimming pools with heated water in addition to its other therapeutic facilities; another public pool, the Lido, is near the soccer stadium on the western outskirts. Tennis can be played on the public courts, some of them covered, near the racecourse in the Untermais/Maia Bassa section where the Passer and Etsch Rivers merge.

A Merano specialty since the late nineteenth century is its grape cure. In its orthodox form it consists in eating half a pound or so of the blue, hard-skinned grapes from the vineyards in the surroundings three times a day during four to six weeks in September and October—but few people today have the time and discipline for such a regimen. Plenty of grapes are nevertheless being consumed in the city every autumn; during the rest of the year unfermented grape juice is recommended. Merano physicians who counsel some form of grape cure will also prescribe a supplementary diet according to whether one wants to lose or gain weight, prevent disease, or seek relief from some complaint. Like other miracle treatments, the grape cure is presumed to act beneficially on a wide range of illnesses.

Whether you take the waters or devour grapes, your medical adviser in Merano will also recommend a lot of walking. This, if nothing else, is bound to improve one's well-being. Long strolls on the many pleasant promenades in the city and its surroundings are probably the best cure for many guests.

⁄∿

COSMOPOLITAN AND
HISTORIC

The racecourse, built in 1935, is the setting for the annual Merano Grand Prix, the culminating event of the spa's society season, on the last Sunday in September. On that occasion the grandstand is filled with local worthies and important-looking personages from all over northern Italy, many accompanied by smart and often very young women who parade the latest Milan fashions. The winning horses bring huge prizes to the holders of the tickets linked with them in a national lottery.

For the visitor to Merano who is dazzled by the many hotels, the almost subtropical exuberance of the parks and gardens, the opulence of the stores and boutiques on the central Corso Libertà/ Freiheitsstrasse, and the cosmopolitan crowd on the promenades, it may take some time to discover the Old Town. Make a beeline to the old Parish Church of St. Nicholas, improperly called also the "Cathedral," whose Gothic steeple with its octagonal Baroque top is visible above the roofscape from many points in the city. The church, dating from the late fourteenth century, is the core of historic Merano, nestling at the foot of a green hill north of the torrent's right bank. The Cathedral's tower, 272 feet (83 meters) tall, is a landmark that appears particularly conspicuous on old pictures representing Merano before it became a spa. Gothic frescoes adorn the steeple's basis. The much smaller Gothic Church of St. Barbara stands on Parish Square at a few yards' distance from the choir of the Cathedral.

Like Bolzano, the province's second city too has its arcaded Laubengasse/Via Portici and Kornmarkt/Piazza del Grano. They are west of the Cathedral and, as in Bolzano, are often crowded with shoppers and tourists. A passage, Via Galilei, from the north side of Laubengasse, leads to the old Town Hall and the so-called Princely Castle. The latter isn't what you would call a castle; rather, it's a simple medieval building with battlements and a tower. It has an interesting history.

Duke Sigismund of Tyrol, a prince of a Hapsburg sideline, had it adapted for himself and his wife around 1450. Sigismund's consort, Eleanor, was one of the daughters of James I, the king of Scotland who was also a poet; the coats of arms of the House of Austria and of Scotland are above the door to the princely sleeping quarters. The building, which may be visited, contains authentic-looking Gothic furniture, medieval weapons, tiled stoves, murals picturing hunting scenes, and a frescoed chapel. Near the chapel are the so-called Emperor Rooms, both with bow windows and wood paneling. Emperor Maximilian I, a distant relative of Sigismund, used them during sojourns in Merano.

Behind the Princely Castle, on the curving Via Galilei, is the Civic Museum. Its prehistoric exhibits include menhirs—upright single-stone monuments with marks and patterns engraved on them—found at a site near Merano that is believed to have been dedicated to Bronze Age cults. There are also old musical instruments, samples of local handicrafts, and works by artists who were natives of this part of the Tyrol or were associated in some way with Merano.

Between the Old Town and the Passer torrent is the Merano of the belle époque. Outstanding buildings are the Civic Theater, opened in 1900, and the domed Municipal Casino (1914), with a thousand-seat auditorium and other halls in which concerts and meetings are held. Both the theater and the casino are in the *Jugendstil* (art nouveau) architecture of the pre–World War I era.

A feeling that time has stood still since then is reinforced when the civic band strikes up Strauss waltzes and Viennese operetta tunes on the embankment in front of the casino in the late morning on many days around the year. Youngsters in blue jeans whom their parents have dragged to Merano and to the palms and flower banks near the bandstand roll up their eyes and snort on hearing the golden oldies and seeing aged people sauntering up and down.

Obermais and Untermais (Maia Alta and Maia Bassa) south of the torrent are today quiet, elegant neighborhoods with hotels, boardinghouses, and private villas amid gardens. The two districts were already inhabited in prehistoric times as many archaeological finds prove and were the site of the ancient Roman town of Maia (the name is probably pre-Roman). A century ago Upper and Lower Maia were a district of vineyards and a few aristocratic mansions; then a building rush set in.

Walking from the Municipal Casino along the Passer embankment a little upstream, the stroller reaches the Winter Promenade, a covered and arcaded walk overgrown with clematis and wisteria. Opposite, on the left bank, is the Summer Promenade, bordered with tall poplars and evergreens. Tulips and other flowers grow at the foot of the white monument of Empress Elisabeth of Austria-Hungary. It shows a youthful "Sissy" seated, with a little crown on her head and a closed book—verses by her beloved Heinrich Heine, no doubt—on her lap. Only her first name, Elisabeth, is engraved on the marble base. Emperor Franz Joseph's Bavarian-born wife sojourned in Merano in 1870 when she was about to begin her restless wanderings all over Europe until an anarchist would stab her to death in Geneva twenty-eight years later. Her long, exhausting walks in Merano's environs became legendary.

Empress Elisabeth's visit to Merano helped make the place fashionable. German and Belgian royalty followed her example, Emperor Franz Joseph came, and aristocrats as well as rich commoners from all over central Europe began flocking to the spa. Soon direct railroad trains brought visitors from Vienna and Budapest. New hotels and villas went up in what had become one of the leading Continental resorts of the Victorian age.

જ્જ

FREUD AND KAFKA AT THE SPA

The Freuds of Vienna too became habitués of Merano. To the founder of psychoanalysis and his family, their summer vacations were always an important project that had to be thoroughly discussed months earlier. When Sigmund Freud's wife felt fatigued in 1898, the decision was taken that she needed a long rest in Merano. Dr. Freud himself and his sister-in-law, Minna Barnays, meanwhile traveled to Switzerland and northern Italy.

The two would tour South Tyrol and adjacent areas also in later years, until it was Minna's turn to spend some time in Merano to recover from what may have been a slight brush with tuberculosis. Freud's travels with his sister-in-law—they would also visit Rome together in 1907—inevitably fed gossip. Minna was four years younger than Martha, Freud's wife, but from photos and descriptions by contemporaries doesn't seem to have been as attractive, and in later years she grew heavy. Martha, however, showed much more interest in Freud's work than did his own wife and was known for her funny observations. Carl Gustav Jung, the Swiss psychiatrist who once had been Freud's friend and associate in the psychoanalytical movement, asserted after their break that Minna Barnays on first meeting him in the Freud home in Vienna had confided to him she and her brother-in-law were having an affair. Ernest Jones, who was close to Freud until the end, dismissed the rumors as "sheer nonsense" in his biography of the master.

Freud's pet daughter, Anna, spent five months in a Merano pension, 1912–13, and celebrated her seventeenth birthday there. Her father had found she needed a long rest after two traumatic experiences in her young life: one was the Matura, the dreaded high school graduation exams that she had passed with flying colors in the Cottage Lyceum in a posh section of Vienna; furthermore, she was recovering from an appendectomy.

Anna dutifully wrote home almost every day, reporting happily whenever the scales showed she had gained a little weight.

The young woman, who herself would one day become an influential psychoanalyst, for the first time read her father's books systematically in Merano. Later she would attend his lectures at Vienna University and undergo analysis by him.

It was in Merano too that one of the twentieth century's celebrated epistolary romances started. Franz Kafka arrived in the South Tyrolean resort, on sick leave from his job at the Workers' Accident Insurance Institute in Prague, early in April 1920. He stayed for three days in the Hotel Emma, a large establishment near the railroad station (which recently was to a large extent converted into an office building) and at once looked for a small family pension. To his sister he wrote he found Merano "incomparably freer, vaster, more varied, more grandiose, with much purer air and a stronger sun" than any vacation spots closer to home.

The writer who was usually agonizing with indecisiveness quickly found a suitable pension, Ottoburg, in the Untermais/ Maia Bassa section, which was run by the wife of a bookstore owner, "very jolly, with thick and pink cheeks." The landlady, he reported, was "very interested in my vegetarianism, although she shows a complete lack of vegetarian fantasy."

A few days later Kafka wrote to "Dear Mrs. Milena"— Milena Jesenská, the twenty-four-year-old wife of a Prague friend of his, Ernest Polak. The couple had recently moved to Vienna, and Milena had translated some of Kafka's stories, including "The Metamorphosis," from the original German into Czech. She had exchanged a few letters with the author, and they had once met with other people present but hadn't talked much.

In his first letter from Merano, signed "F. Kafka," the writer in uncharacteristic cheerfulness reported that "I live here pretty well, the mortal body could hardly stand more; the balcony of my room is immersed in a garden, surrounded by flowering shrubs (the vegetation here is strange, in weather in which in Prague the puddles practically freeze over the flowers slowly open in front of my balcony)." Kafka added that "I so much wish you could be in Meran." Recently, he recalled, she had written him about not being able to breathe—"image and meaning are very close in this word, and in Meran both might become a little easier." The writer always gave the city its German name, Meran.

Soon Kafka and Milena used first names in the letters and telegrams they sent each other, sometimes more than one a day. "What a country this is!" he wrote. "Heavens, Milena, if only you were here . . ." Later: "There are beautiful ruins everywhere on the mountains, and one ought to become as beautiful too."

Kafka's sick leave expired at the end of May 1920, but since he was entitled to five weeks' paid vacation, he requested and obtained permission from his office to stay until the end of June. His letters to Milena became increasingly passionate and revelatory. He discussed with her his own Jewishness (Milena was the gentile wife of a Jewish intellectual) and other personal matters, like his relationship with his father. Milena's replies are lost; they were probably destroyed later by Kafka.

From Merano Kafka made a trip to Bolzano with an acquaintance from the pension, a friendly engineer, and in Klobenstein/ Collalbo above the regional capital "breathed, although not quite in my right mind, pure, almost cold air in front of the first chain of the Dolomites." After three months of rest and a vegetarian diet with plenty of milk, he had gained six pounds in weight, but his left lung was still tuberculous.

On his way home Kafka would spend four days with Milena in Vienna. They would later keep writing and sending telegrams to each other and would have another brief encounter on the

Austrian-Czechoslovak border, but their relationship loosened, and he eventually broke it off. Four years after his stay in Merano the writer died in a private sanatorium at Kierling near Vienna, another young woman, Dora Dymant, at his bedside.

During his long sojourn in Merano, Kafka almost certainly strolled on the Tappeiner Weg, a nearly level walk 500 feet (about 150 meters) above the city. It can be reached from the river promenade by easy paths and commands beautiful views. The walkway, hewn into the rock of the Küchelberg north of Merano, is lined with cypresses, palmettos, and other dense greenery and is adorned with a bust of Dr. Franz Tappeiner on an elaborate pedestal; he was a civic-minded nineteenth-century physician who created the attractive promenade.

෴

A CASTLE AND A NAME

From the Tappeiner Walk a steeper path, the Tirolersteig/Sentiero per Tirolo, leads to the provincial highway up the Küchelberg and to Tirol Village and Castle. Hikers will make the excursion from Merano in one and a half hours, but there are easier ways of getting up there: take the public bus, marked "Dorf Tirol—Tirolo," from the railroad station or drive on National Route 44 into the lower Passeier Valley as far as the turnoff to the provincial highway to Tirol Village. The trip takes fifteen to twenty minutes. Also, a chair lift goes up the Küchelberg from the Via Galilei near the Civic Museum; from its upper terminus walk some twenty minutes to Tirol Village.

The origin of the word *Tirol* or *Tyrol* is controversial; according to one explanation, it goes back to prehistory and means "old path" or "old passage." What is certain is that Tirol Village gave its name to the castle that was built on a nearby height at the beginning of the twelfth century and that eventually the entire Alpine region was called after the castle. For some time whoever was lord of that stronghold was lord of all of Tyrol.

To natives the name has a powerfully emotional, near mythical ring. Old songs and occasional patriotic rhetoric even today express devotion to the "holy land of Tyrol," although the source of such presumed sanctity, despite its strong Christian tradition, is not clear. If one's ancestors have for generations lived in the region, one is likely to feel first and foremost as a Tyrolean rather than an Austrian, German, or Italian. This sense of a separate ethnic-cultural identity seems to have remained undiluted to this day.

Tirol Village, where such sentiments are historically rooted, is today a touristic satellite of Merano, on which it looks down from 1,955 feet (596 meters) above sea level. The tidy village, which is bathed in brilliant sunlight many days around the year, has 2,000 permanent residents and offers 5,300 guest beds in its 160 hotels, pensions, and inns and in private homes.

As a settlement Tirol Village is at least 1,400 years old. The Parish Church of St. John the Baptist dates from the twelfth century and has a Gothic choir from the fourteenth century. It contains noteworthy Gothic wood carvings.

The old Romanesque steeple was in the seventeenth century heightened with an octagonal top copying the tower crown of the Merano parish church.

The roaring tourist business of the last few years has unfortunately led to overbuilding. Around the old farmhouses and inns new hotels, pensions, cafes, and stores compete today for patronage by the many thousands of visitors who flock to the village from April to the end of October. Dorf Tirol (Tyrol Village) has a public outdoor swimming pool and is at the center of a network of promenades and walking paths across vineyards and orchards.

The much frequented Falknerweg (Falconers' Path) along the edge of a ravine leads to Tyrol Castle. The historic stronghold can be reached from the village only on foot, in about twenty minutes. The visitor must pass a 260-foot (80-meter) tunnel, built in the seventeenth century, and then walk over a short viaduct. Earth pyramids like the "Crowned Girls" on the Ritten/Renon high plateau near Bolzano can be seen on the right side.

The castle, at 2,096 feet (639 meters) altitude, sits atop a steep hill consisting of the debris of an Ice Age moraine. The counts of the Vinschgau—the Etsch/Adige Valley west of Merano—had the fortress erected around 1140, took up residence in it, and from then called themselves counts of Tyrol. Dante mentioned the castle and the Alpine area it controlled as "Tiralli" in the *Inferno* (XX, 62–63), a geographical reference to explain the location of Lake Garda.

The Tyrol family became extinct in the male line in 1335, and the last heiress, Margaret Maultasch ("Pocket Mouth"), a famously unattractive and astute lady who married twice, abdicated in 1363 in favor of the House of Hapsburg.

Tyrol Castle decayed, and in 1640 a part of it crashed into the ravine in a landslide. The near ruin was a possession of the emperor of Austria-Hungary until 1918, then became a property of the Italian state, and in 1973 was transferred by it to the autonomous province of Bolzano/Südtirol. The regional government had it thoroughly restored and designated it as an archaeological, historic, and art museum. It is open to visitors daily except Monday.

The porch and doorway leading into the vast Hall of Knights

and the portal of the adjacent chapel are in Romanesque style, clearly inspired by Lombard models. The damaged frescoes of the chapel include a coat of arms with what is said to be the oldest colored representation of the Red Eagle, the totem of Tyrol. The west windows of the castle's main building command a much admired view of the Etsch/Adige Valley.

The exhibits in the castle's archaeological collection illustrate what is known about the Stone, Copper, Bronze, and Iron Ages in this part of the Alps, the civilization of the Rhaetian inhabitants, the Roman period, the coming of Christianity, and the area's takeover by Germanic tribes. The other sections of the museum trace Tyrolean history from the early Middle Ages to the present and contain significant works of art.

❧

A Poet's Refuge

Also noteworthy, for a variety of reasons, is the multiturreted Brunnenburg (Well Castle), perched on a hill of glacial rock fragments below Tyrol Castle and separated from it by the ravine. Walk from Tirol Village along the Falconers' Path as far as a turnoff on your left with the sign "Brunnenburg." A steep lane through orchards descends, past an old millhouse, to a bizarre structure with towers, terraces, and concrete balconies. The core of the building was commissioned around 1250 by an official of the counts of Tyrol, apparently to serve both as his own residence and as a watchtower and outer defense position of his masters' castle higher up.

Through the centuries the Well Castle was used as a mansion and later as a farmhouse. It had long become dilapidated when a rich German, Karl Schwickert from Pforzheim in the state of Baden, bought it in 1903. He not only wanted to live in the building, but, being a Freemason, planned to convert it into a Masonic temple as well. He had the old edifice transformed into a fake-romantic fantasy, shunning no expense. He called it the Wasserschloss (Water Castle).

In 1904 Schwickert's wife, Maria, fell to her death from one of the high balconies. People in Tirol Village were convinced the new owner of the Brunnenburg had pushed her down, but the authorities accepted his version that she had suffered a spell of dizziness while watering flowers and ruled that Mrs. Schwickert had died accidentally. After World War I Italy seized the Brunnen-burg together with Tyrol Castle but allowed its former owner, by then an eccentric and lonely old man, to live on in it; he died in 1925.

The Brunnenburg remained vacant for many years, decaying again for lack of maintenance. It had become a haunted house, so the story in Tirol Village and in Merano went, but it is more likely that mice and the occasional squatter rather than the ghosts of medieval personages or of the unfortunate Mrs. Schwickert were dwelling in the weird shell.

In 1948 the illegitimate daughter of Ezra Pound, Mary Rudge, and her husband, Boris de Rachewiltz Baratti, scratched together enough money to buy the ruin. (For Mary's early story, see page 143.) They and their children first lived in a few rooms on top of the building, then over the following years gradually restored the other rooms and halls on six lower levels and started taking in paying guests.

In 1958 Ezra Pound found a haven at the Brunnenburg after his release from St. Elisabeths, the mental hospital in Washington, D.C., where he had been held. The poet who had made pro-

Fascist broadcasts from Italy during World War II was taken into custody by United States forces at Rapallo on the Italian Riviera in 1945; he spent nearly thirteen years in detention. Archibald MacLeish, Ernest Hemingway, Robert Frost, T. S. Eliot, and other literary figures appealed to the United States government to dismiss the case against Pound, and the secretary general of the United Nations, Dag Hammarskjöld, backed the petition.

When Pound arrived at the Brunnenburg after disembarking in Genoa, he met for the first time his grandchildren, Siegfried Walter and Patrizia Barbara. From the Washington psychiatric institution he had chosen the "Walter" for his grandson as a tribute to Walther von der Vogelweide.

At the Brunnenburg the American poet trimmed the shrubbery in the garden with large shears and had five hundred new vines planted on the slope below the building, although during excursions around the neighborhood he had told vintners they could make more money by planting soybeans instead of growing wine.

Still as a detainee in Washington, Pound had sent two hundred sugar-maple saplings to his daughter and son-in-law so that they should be able to produce their own maple syrup. The trees, however, wouldn't thrive in the soil and climate of Merano, as the poet now could see with his own eyes. Eventually all but one of the maples withered; in 1993 I was shown the last survivor of Pound's trees in the garden on the northwest side of the Brunnenburg.

Hemingway sent a $1,000 check, but Pound gratefully said that luckily he didn't have to cash it and had it mounted in a paperweight. At the Brunnenburg he continued working on his *Cantos*. After a few months he moved to Rapallo and eventually back again to the Brunnenburg. He suffered a psychological breakdown and for some time had to be fed intravenously at the Martinsbrunn Clinic on Merano's northern outskirts. He recovered, flew to London in 1965 for T. S. Eliot's funeral, visited Yeats's widow in Dublin, made a trip to Greece to mark his eightieth birthday, and revisited the United States. Pound died in Venice in 1972; his grave is on the cemetery island of San Michele.

The poet's grandson, Siegfried W. de Rachewiltz, told me that scholars doing research on Pound were often coming to the Brunnenburg and that Pound symposia were occasionally held there. The building, whose official address is 3 Ezra-Pound-Weg, I-39019 Dorf Tirol, Italy, also houses a Pound library.

But the Brunnenburg today is above all a private agricultural museum, which Dr. de Rachewiltz, an ethnologist, has organized. It focuses on grain growing and milling and bread making and has various old farming implements and bakery equipment on display. Antiquated machinery is used to demonstrate the traditional methods of Tyrolean vintners, beekeepers, carpenters, weavers, and sundry artisans. The Brunnenburg Museum is open to visitors daily except Tuesday from the beginning of April to the end of October.

∽

HERO OF TYROL

Beyond the turnoff to Tirol Village, the highway from Merano, National Route 44, runs through orchards and between terraced vineyards in the broad lower valley of the Passer/Passirio torrent. The vineyards end near the village of Riffian/Rifiano, a regional pilgrimage center. Its Baroque parish church from the seventeenth century amid a small cluster of old houses, surrounded by rows of vines on the slopes, contains a much venerated image of the grieving Madonna, painted around 1400, and many old and modern votive tablets.

Higher up, about half a mile (not quite a kilometer) southwest of Riffian, is Kuens, with its about two hundred inhabitants the smallest municipality of South Tyrol. The curious coat of arms of the little village shows the bearded eighth-century missionary bishop St. Corbinian from Bavaria with his crosier marching together with a friendly bear that carries a backpack. St. Corbinian is credited with having founded Kuens. The village church goes back to the High Middle Ages; a few frescoes from the fourteenth century are still visible on the south wall.

Proceeding on Highway 44, the traveler comes to the area of the Shield Farms. Schildhof (Shield Court) was the name for a farmstead whose owner had received hereditary freehold privileges from the count of Tyrol in exchange for certain semifeudal duties: he had to do military service with a sword and shield (whence the name) in times of war and to attend the lord at his castle on some occasions. The shield farmers were allowed to fortify their houses with battlements and turrets but had to refrain from erecting veritable castles for themselves even though they might have had the money to do so. Ten or twelve sturdy shield houses have survived, some as hotels.

Ten miles (16 kilometers) north of Merano the road approaches the places where Andreas Hofer (1767–1810), the Tyrolean hero, was born and captured. One mile (1.6 kilometers) beyond the village of St. Martin is the Sandhof on the left bank of the Passer torrent, where Hofer's father owned and managed an inn "at the sandbank." Andreas inherited the property, the business, and the nickname "Sandwirt" (Host at the Sand). The bearded innkeeper who also traded in cattle and wine is described as a cheerful and honest man who had taken part as a sharpshooter and captain of the Tyrolean militia in Austria's wars against revolutionary France between 1796 and 1805 and therefore had some understanding of military tactics. He always wore Tyrolean peasant clothes with a broad-brimmed hat.

After Napoleon's victory at Austerlitz the Austrian government ceded the Tyrol to his ally, Bavaria, in the Treaty of Pressburg in 1805. The Bavarians turned out to be stern masters; they banned the ancient name Tyrol, substituting "Southern Bavaria" for it, and made themselves unpopular in their newly won Alpine territory in many ways. When Austria renewed fighting against Napoleon in 1809, Hofer (who had visited Vienna the year before) led an uprising against the hated Bavarians. His call to arms—"Men, it's time!"—has remained proverbial all over Tyrol to this day and is often used on all kinds of occasions.

Hofer's peasant forces defeated the Bavarians in various engagements, and the Austrian troops were able to reoccupy Innsbruck. In an armistice with Napoleon the Austrian emperor, Franz I, yielded Tyrol again, and French-Bavarian troops once more took possession of the country. Hofer led another rebellion, inflicting heavy casualties on the Napoleonic forces under Marshal François-Joseph Lefebvre, the duke of Danzig, and conquered Innsbruck with his irregulars. Elected commander-in-chief by the Tyroleans, he ruled Tyrol on behalf of the emperor for two months.

In October 1808, however, Emperor Franz I ceded Tyrol to Bavaria for the third time in the Treaty of Schönbrunn, betraying Hofer's trust. Hofer, the unwavering Hapsburg loyalist, started yet another uprising, but his forces were beaten in an ultimate battle on the Isel hill south of Innsbruck. Long declared an outlaw by both the French and the Bavarians, Hofer withdrew to his native Passer Valley and hid in a hut at 4,728 feet (1,441 meters) altitude above St. Martin. A local farmer named Raffl betrayed the hero's refuge to the Bavarians, earning himself prize money, a pension, and asylum in Upper Bavaria as well as vituperation as the "Judas of Tyrol" by his own countrymen. Hofer's hiding place used to draw many visitors until 1920, when it burned down.

The French detained Hofer, transferred him to Mantua, and on Napoleon's direct orders shot him there in February 1810. The Tyrolean patriot died with dignity—in fact, after the first salvo from the nervous execution detail he is said to have chided them for their bad marksmanship. His remains were transferred from Mantua to the Franciscan Church in Innsbruck in 1823.

Generations of Austrian schoolchildren have sung an 1836 ballad by the writer Julius Moser (1803–67), telling how Hofer, who so often had brought death to enemies in the "Holy Land of Tyrol," faced death himself with courage, refusing to have his eyes bandaged, personally commanding, "Fire!" and exclaiming, "Alas, how badly you shoot! Good-bye, my land, Tyrol!" I still know by heart many of the verses, which we had to learn in elementary school. They start with the lines "At Mantua, in fetters / The faithful Hofer was . . ." In Tyrol, south and north of the Brenner Pass, the "Andreas Hofer Song" is something of a national anthem, always played and chanted on festive or patriotic occasions, especially on the anniversary of the hero's death on February 20.

The Sandwirt House on the Passer torrent is today a much frequented restaurant. Adjacent to Hofer's whitewashed, gabled birthplace are a small museum with relics reminiscent of the hero and the events of 1809 and a chapel that Hofer's grandfather had built. Nearby is another memorial, erected in 1899, with murals of 1809 war scenes.

At the cemetery of St. Leonhard, a little more than a mile (almost two kilometers) north of Hofer's birthplace, is the tomb of his wife, Anna Ladurner. She survived him by sixteen years. Outside the village is a second cemetery with the graves of 230 French soldiers who died during fighting in the valley in 1809 in this corner of the Alps, a small but nevertheless impressive part of the hecatombs who were slaughtered during the Napoleonic years.

From St. Leonhard the highway climbs in many switchbacks over 12.5 miles (20 kilometers) to the Jaufenpass/Passo del Giovo, which is 6,870 feet (2,094 meters) high. This Alpine passageway was much traveled before the direct Brenner highway to Bolzano through the Eisack/Isarco gorges and eventually the Brenner railroad were built. The old name of the pass may be derived from Jupiter or from the Latin term for yoke (*iugum*), or else it may go back to some pre-Roman root. The views from the Jaufenpass, above the treeline, are grandiose: glaciers, harsh rock walls, lofty peaks, and snowy Alpine ridges are all around. Route 44 descends in another series of bends across pine forests and eventually reaches the green fields near Sterzing/Vipiteno.

༄

RHAETIAN VALLEY

The upper reaches of the Etsch/Adige River west and northwest of Merano are known as the Vinschgau/Val Venosta. It is a broad, natural trough hollowed out by Ice Age glaciers, bordered on either side by high mountains with few foothills. Prehistoric

Ligurians and Illyrians, Celtic invaders, Roman legions, Teutonic tribes, and plenty of medieval and modern soldiery passed through it.

Today the valley provides road connections with Lombardy and Milan across the lofty Stilfser Joch/Passo Stelvio, to the Swiss Engadin and St. Moritz by way of the Müstair Valley, and to the Austrian Inn Valley across the Reschenpass/Passo di Resia. The upper Etsch/Adige has long been canalized for extended stretches; thus vast alluvial areas that in the past were regularly flooded became fertile farmland.

Woods are less dense in the Vinschgau and the climate is drier than in most other parts of South Tyrol. The northern slopes are warmer than the mountains on the opposite side of the valley because they get more sunshine. Settlers have since the earliest times built elaborate networks of canals to bring the waters from glaciers and snow fields to their farms and gardens. These canals are locally called *Waale* (singular: *Waal*), a term probably derived from the Latin word *aqualis* (water-). Maintenance of the *Waal* system was continuous throughout the millennia, until modern irrigation methods and sprinklers replaced the ancient canals almost everywhere. Some of the *Waale*, however, can still be seen, and hikers love to follow the paths along their course on the slopes.

Many place names in the Vinschgau/Val Venosta echo the language of the Celtic-Illyrian inhabitants whom the conquering Romans found and whom they called Rhaetians. In the spring of 15 B.C. Nero Claudius Drusus, stepson of Emperor Augustus, subdued the tribe of the Venosti in the upper Etsch/Adige Valley; the Italian Val Venosta and the German Vinschgau are both derived from the Latin appellation *Venosti*. A few months after the spring campaign Drusus was joined by his older brother,

Tiberius, who had been engaged in military operations on the Rhine. The two divided their forces, Tiberius marching up the Etsch/Adige Valley and Drusus up the Eisack/Isarco Valley to and beyond the Brenner Pass. In the Inn Valley the brothers united their troops again and proceeded to claim much land between the Alps and the Danube for Rome.

As in all conquered territories, the Roman engineers at once started building roads. The military route from the confluence of the Etsch and the Eisack to the Reschen/Resia Pass and beyond came to be known as the Via Claudia Augusta; one of its ancient milestones can be seen in the Civic Museum of Bolzano. Today's National Routes 38 (Bolzano-Merano-Spondigna) and 40 (Spondigna-Reschen/Resia Pass) essentially follow the ancient Roman road the entire 66 miles (105 kilometers) to the Italian-Austrian border.

The neat railroad station of Merano always saddens me. It was there that I saw my father for the last time when he returned to Vienna at the end of a vacation we had spent together. He died suddenly soon afterward while I was in the United States. We had agreed on Merano as our base for car trips all over South Tyrol and the Dolomites, where my father had been a soldier during World War I. I also took him across the Jaufenpass to Sterzing/Vipiteno to have him meet my mother-in-law. It was the first time (and was to be also the last), and the two took a great liking to each other. I introduced my father also to Luise, the owner of the Maibad Inn, where I had stayed during my first visit. Father was enchanted and asked, "Why didn't you make this our headquarters instead of that fancy hotel in Merano?"

In 1993 I asked a railroad employee at the Merano station why there was no longer a train to Mals, a town 35 miles (56 kilometers) up the valley. An Italian, he grinned and said: "We are lucky to still have trains from Bolzano to Merano; the state railways would be happy to end passenger service on this section, too. Everybody in the Val Venosta has a car. They make a lot of money with the tourists and with the apples and pears they grow and sell directly to supermarket chains in Germany. But you should try their apricots!" The frost-resistant Vinschgau apricot trees indeed produce fruits that are famous all over the region. They are smaller than the rather flavorless apricots one usually gets at markets but have an aroma and taste that to me bring back childhood memories of similar fruit from the sunny Wachau Valley on the Danube upstream of Vienna. Throughout the Vinschgau/Val Venosta vines were torn out during the second half of the twentieth century and old vineyards were transformed into orchards or fruit plantations. It's not a great loss because the wines grown in the valley were never very good.

As for the railroad, ecological awareness has lately prompted plans to improve the tracks and reactivate the line from Merano to Mals at some future time. Until then, bus service is the only public transport in the upper Adige/Etsch Valley.

※

TYPEWRITERS AND
A CATTLE SHRINE

Coming from the east, the traveler, passing turnoffs to prosperous-looking hamlets in the broad, green river plain, sees castles on the heights on both sides of the highway. A little more than 4 miles (7 kilometers) out of Merano is a village with a Rhaetian name, Partschins (Italianized into Parcines), the birthplace of one of the pioneers of the typewriter.

He was Peter Mitterhofer (1822–1893), a carpenter and cabinetmaker who liked to tinker and was something of a loner. In 1864 he built a thirty-key writing machine, mainly of wood with a few metal parts. He later turned out improved models, and major encyclopedias list him as one of several mechanics in various countries who produced early writing devices. Tyroleans, not surprisingly, call him the "inventor of the typewriter."

Mitterhofer was granted small subsidies by the imperial government in Vienna, which showed mild interest in his machines, but nothing came of this invention. The first efficient typewriter, based on an 1868 patent obtained by Christopher L. Sholes and Carlos Glidden of Milwaukee, Wisconsin, was manufactured by the Remington firm of Ilion, New York, in 1874.

Partschins opened a Mitterhofer Museum in the former grade school in the riverside hamlet of Töll in 1993, the centenary of the inventor's death, and plans to transfer it to a new building near the village center. The collection shows the development of mechanical writing from rudimentary contraptions to the latest electronic models; its creator, Ewald Lassnig, a retired schoolteacher who wrote a Mitterhofer biography, said that Partschins now had the world's seventeenth typewriter museum. The Austrian postal administration issued a Mitterhofer memorial mail stamp.

Six miles (10 kilometers) west of Partschins is the valley's first major village, Naturns/Natorno. It lies on the left (north) bank below a medieval castle with two towers, now a pension. There are more than seventy other hotels and boardinghouses in the village and its surroundings.

An ancient little church standing in isolation in the fields northeast of Naturns is one of South Tyrol's monuments of early Christianity and early-medieval art. The edifice, about fifteen by fifteen feet (five by five meters), with a square Romanesque steeple, is dedicated to St. Proculus, bishop of Verona, who is revered locally as patron saint of cattle. Some scholars assume that farmers used to drive their oxen and cows to the spot for benedictions and prayers even before the shrine was built in the seventh century. At that time the people in the valley and on the nearby slopes must still have spoken their Rhaetian vernacular, probably mingling it with Latin phrases picked up from the Roman legionnaires and officials.

The old sanctuary, which is surrounded by a low wall, became a major attraction in 1925 after undistinguished paintings in the interior had been removed, and eighth-century frescoes came to light. Although in part damaged by mortar patches that fill cracks, the murals still surprise by their naive designs, suggesting pictures made by modern children, and by their fresh colors (except the fading blues). A saint with a halo—St. Proculus?—is shown on what looks like a swing but may represent a device on ropes to descend from a wall while other figures look on. The scene may depict the saintly bishop's flight from Verona, where adversaries had been harassing him. The fresco on the western wall of the small church represents a procession of a dozen head of cattle with a vigilant dog and what little has remained of two figures of cowherds. The picture clearly fixes a scene that must have been often repeated on that spot. Two elongated angels are recognizable on the east wall behind the altar.

Experts have detected similarities between the murals of Naturns and the art of Irish monks who illuminated manuscripts with miniatures and ornaments. One theory is that a painter-monk from St. Gall in neighboring Switzerland, then a center of Irish-Scottish missionary activity, decorated the Church of St. Proculus.

From a power plant west of Naturns a secondary road follows the bed of the Schnals/Senales torrent, which furnishes water from the high glaciers and the snow drifts for the turbines. Through this side valley, 5,300 years ago, the Iceman (chapter 2) may have climbed to Mount Similaun, where death was awaiting him. The Schnals/Senales Valley is a wild gorge in its lower stretch; higher up it widens, affording splendid views of the Similaun. The village of Karthaus/Certosa, named after a former charterhouse (monastery), at 4,341 feet (1,323 meters) altitude, is the administrative center of a cluster of hamlets and some thirty hotels and inns whose guests come for skiing vacations around the year; they can practice on the glaciers in both summer and winter. One of the hamlets is called Unserfrau/Madonna; the Simons from Nuremberg stayed there before and after their ascent of Mount Similaun during which they discovered the Iceman.

The highest hotels are above Vernagt on an artificial lake at 5,328 feet (1,624 meters) altitude. Even higher up are a few mountain farms, which are the loftiest in all of South Tyrol, and the Similaun Refuge (page 36), where the first news of the Iceman originated.

❧

HAIRPIN BENDS

Proceeding westward from Naturns in the main valley, one passes several medieval strongholds, including Kastelbell, a ruined thirteenth-century structure that looks as if it had grown out of the steep rock above the highway. The little town of Schlanders/Silandro, 6 miles (10 kilometers) to the west, is dominated by another castle and has an interesting sixteenth-century church with a 300-foot (91-meter) belltower as well as frescoes by the Vienna court painter Adam Josef von Mölkh (1695–1770). Some battlemented old houses contribute to the town's moody atmosphere.

The highway rises, passing the village of Laas/Lasa and its famous marble quarries. Since the fifteenth century, the fine-grained, white, weather-resistant Laas marble has been widely used throughout the region (including the Walther-von-der-Vogelweide statue in Bolzano) and in buildings and for monuments all over Europe.

The upper Etsch/Adige Valley broadens again, and the road offers vistas of the Ortler/Ortles Group, the highest mountain massif of South Tyrol, rising to 12,802 feet (3,902 meters) above sea level, with scores of glaciers.

National Route 38, which will cross the Ortler at the Passo dello Stelvio/Stilfser Joch, turns southward at the village of Spondinig/Spondigna, 30 miles (48 kilometers) west of Merano. The highway continuing to the headwaters of the Etsch/Adige is National Route 40. The Stelvio Pass Road is one of Europe's loftiest motor routes, regularly made impassable by snow from October to June. It was built from 1820 to 1824 on orders from Emperor Franz I in Vienna to enable his troops to be moved from Tyrol into Lombardy, then an Austrian possession. During World War I Austrio-Hungarian and Italian soldiers faced each other across the glaciers and fought from positions amid ice and snow at more than 10,000 feet (3,000 meters) above sea level.

The highway passes the Etsch/Adige and climbs the foothills. At the hamlet of Gomagoi, a Romansh name meaning Twin Waters, a turnoff leads to the road up the Suldental/Val di Solda. The village of Sulden/Solda, 6,053 feet (1,844 meters) high, with many hotels and pensions, is a base for mountaineering in the Ortler massif and for exertion in the Ortler ski circus with its many funiculars, ski lifts, and pistes. There are a dozen refuges on various heights.

National Route 38 gets steeper beyond Gomagoi. It approaches the sheltered village of Trafoi (Three Fountains), which affords magnificent views of the Ortler and the forested slopes on either side of the valley. From Trafoi, at an altitude of 5,056 feet (1,541 meters), Route 38 rises in forty-eight numbered hairpin curves above the treeline to the Stelvio Pass/Stilfser Joch, 9,045 feet (2,757 meters) above sea level. Sturdy types may climb to the pass from Trafoi over shortcuts in more than two hours, but the views of the snowy peaks are better from the motor road.

The panorama from the pass is overwhelming. A few hotels on the nearby slopes look down on the pass road; they are closed in winter because the Stelvio is a place for summer skiing and is abandoned in the cold months.

A steep footpath from the pass road leads in twenty minutes of strenuous climbing to the Three-Language Peak/Pizzo Garibaldi, 9,325 feet (2,842 meters) high. Until 1918 it was the point where the borders of Austria-Hungary, Italy, and Switzerland converged; now it marks the Italian-Swiss frontier. The three languages spoken in the areas below the summit are German, Italian, and Romansh.

The Stelvio Pass and Sulden/Solda are both in the Stelvio National Park, which was created in 1935. The largest nature reservation in the western Alps, it spreads over 386 square miles (954 square kilometers) of mountainscape with more than one hundred glaciers in the Italian provinces of Bolzano, Sondrio, and Trento. Ibexes, deer, and other mountain fauna thrive in the park, in which hunting and fishing, of course, are banned. Tent camping is forbidden, and vehicles with trailers and campers must move on.

The west ramp of the Stelvio Pass Road, with many tunnels and superimposed, terracelike bends, is less spectacular than the ascent from the Vinschgau/Val Venosta. The first town in the Valtellina is Bormio, 12 miles (19 kilometers) from the pass; the motor trip from the Stelvio Pass to Milan, 140 miles (224 kilometers) by way of Bormio, will take three hours if traffic isn't too heavy.

✑

WALLED COW TOWN

Straight ahead on the Vinschgau/Val Venosta highway (National Route 40), 2.5 miles (4 kilometers) past the Stelvio Road turnoff, lies the old village of Schluderns/Sluderno. Situated in a wide basin, the village lies below the Churburg, a well-preserved castle complex 3,264 feet (995 meters) above sea level, which the bishops of Chur in Switzerland built in the thirteenth century.

The vast, yellow-gray structures with their massive keep, towers, walls, battlements, and outworks were later transformed into a splendid Renaissance mansion, which has belonged to the Counts Trapp, an old South Tyrolean aristocratic family, since the sixteenth century. Their castle can be visited daily except Monday from March to October, and it's a worthwhile trip. Its attractions include the Trapps' vaulted hall filled with medieval armor and an arcaded courtyard with two-story frescoed loggias.

One and a half miles (2 kilometers) from Schluderns/Sluderno on Route 39 is South Tyrol's smallest town, Glurns/Glorenza.

Completely surrounded by five-hundred-year-old walls and towers amid fields, it has fewer than eight hundred residents; some of them still keep cattle and do rural work, but many now commute to jobs in nearby Switzerland during the week. However, off the main street with its solid, arcaded houses and the central square, a cow-town atmosphere lingers—if you are looking for quaintness, Glurns/Glorenza amply provides it. The Gothic parish church, just outside the walls and beyond the Etsch/ Adige River, has a remarkable Last Judgment fresco from 1496 on its steeple below a large clock and an onion dome. The tall church tower, the town's red roofscape, the gray walls, and the neat green-and-yellow fields blend into a enchanting panorama.

National Route 39 continues to the Italian-Swiss frontier post near the village of Taufers/Tubre, 4,042 feet (1,232 meters) above sea level. There are two ruined castles in the village, as well as a Romanesque church, St. John's, which contains a late-twelfth-century fresco of St. Christopher carrying an adult-looking but diminutive Jesus, who is shown in the gesture of blessing. Art historians say it is one of the oldest representations of the saint.

The first village in Switzerland's Canton Graubünden/Gri-sons is Müstair. The Romansh name means "monastery"—the ancient Benedictine abbey of St. John the Baptist just north of the village. Charlemagne is said to have founded Müstair between 780 and 790, and a stucco statue of the great ruler with a crown on his head, his hands holding scepter and orb, has the place of honor in its church. The abbey became a Benedictine nunnery in the twelfth century, and the nuns are still there, practicing their widely renowned skills of fine embroidery.

UNESCO, the United Nations Educational, Scientific, and Cultural Organization, has placed the Müstair convent on its list of outstanding monuments of humankind's cultural patrimony. This is essentially because of the frescoes dating from the Carolingian period (eighth to tenth centuries) that were in the church. Most of them have been detached and can now be seen in the Swiss National Museum in Zurich, but other murals from the twelfth century, discovered after World War II, have remained there, best preserved on the church's north wall.

Many persons in Müstair and in Santa Maria, the population center of the Müstair Valley, at an altitude of 4,511 feet (1,375 meters) 2.5 miles (4 kilometers) southwest of the abbey village, as well as the mountaineers in the nearby hamlets, speak Romansh, one of the four national languages of the Swiss Confederation. The other three national languages are German, French, and Italian.

The tongue of Grischs (Grisons), a branch of what scholars call the Rhaeto-Romance linguistic family, was once common in the Vinschgau/Val Venosta, as place names like Glurns and Schluderns betray. The language became extinct in the Etsch/Adige Valley after the Teutonic invasions; idioms similar to Romansh are the Ladin spoken in the Val Gardena and side valleys (chapter 7) and the Friulan of the Dolomites.

From Santa Maria, Swiss Route 66 climbs and bends over about 12 miles (20 kilometers) to the Stelvio Pass. The Swiss-Italian border post is below the Three-Language Peak (see page 103) at the Umbrail Pass, 8,205 feet (2,501 meters) above sea level. The road is closed between November and June.

Swiss Route 28 to Zernez and St. Moritz in the Engadin Valley crosses the Swiss National Park beyond the Fuorn/Ofen (Furnace) Pass, which is 7,050 feet (2,149 meters) above sea level. The nature reserve covers 67 square miles (168 square kilometers) and can be visited only on foot, except in winter when the entire area is closed.

Travelers who get out of their car or coach at the Fuorn Pass where one of the eleven entrances to the National Park is located will see fallen branches and trees in thick underbrush. Human meddling with nature is strictly banned throughout the vast enclave, which was created in 1914. Ibexes, chamois, and deer roam the reservation, which rises to heights of about 10,200 feet (3,100 meters); birds of many species live in the dense woodland. Visitors must obey rules that are much more stringent than those in the Stelvio National Park—stay on marked paths, refrain from camping or skiing, avoid loud noises. Stiff penalties threaten anyone who picks flowers or mushrooms, captures or kills an animal (if only a beetle), or lights a fire. Dogs must be kept out of the park.

❦

DROWNED VILLAGE

Returning to the Vinschgau/Val Venosta after a trip into the Canton Grisons, you may turn off National Route 41 after Taufers/Tubre and proceed straight to the old market town of Mals/Malles, 2.5 miles (4 kilometers) northwest of Schluderns/Sluderno. The railroad from Bolzano once had its terminus—and may again have it at some future time—at the foot of the slope against which the town, with its five Romanesque and Gothic towers, was built. The small Church of St. Benedict, with its square Romanesque steeple, was once an outpost of the Müstair abbey. It contains ninth-century murals that, together with those of St. Proculus near Naturns/Natorno, belong to the oldest medieval works of art in the region. The Mals frescoes represent Jesus, an opened Bible in his left hand, surrounded by angels, martyrs, and the Carolingian founders of the church.

A side valley opening at the village of Burgeis/Burgusio, about 1 mile (2 kilometers) north of Mals, is dominated by the Benedictine abbey of Marienberg (Mary's Mountain) on a forested rocky spur at an altitude of 4,383 feet (1,336 meters). The large white building on mighty substructures—a little like those of the Dalai Lama's former Potala Palace in Lhasa, Tibet—was founded in 1160. It is also a satellite of the Müstair abbey.

Marienberg abbey is a few minutes from Burgeis/Burgusio by car (over a paved road) or half an hour by foot (over a narrow path). Tours of the vast complex are conducted daily except Saturday afternoon and Sunday. A monastery, a church with a tall steeple, cloisters, a school, auxiliary buildings, and gardens are grouped around a spacious courtyard.

The church, from the twelfth century, was redecorated in the Baroque manner five hundred years later, with plenty of stucco work in the interior. I was struck by the seven-hundred-year-old frescoes in the crypt, some of which were discovered only recently; they show Jesus with the Apostles Peter and Paul and angels, all represented with Byzantine rigidity. The views of the Vinschgau and of parts of the Ortler massif from the abbey are an extra bonus.

From the village of Burgeis/Burgusio it's not quite 10 miles (16 kilometers) to the Italian-Austrian border. Route 40 skirts the picturesque Haidersee/Lago della Muta, a small lake surrounded by forests, and then a much bigger artificial lake, which feeds a power plant near Schluderns/Sluderno downstream. The upper part of a Gothic steeple with faded red clock dials, triple-arch windows, and a pyramid roof sticks out of the water near the highway on the lake's east bank. The often photographed landmark is a remnant of the fourteenth-century Chapel of St. Anne that stood above the village of Graun/Curon, which was flooded when the power dam was built in 1949.

The villagers of old Graun/Curon were resettled in new houses on a slope east of the lake. The transferred village, at an altitude of 4,986 feet (1,520 meters), has a few inns and pensions and is a base for hiking, mountaineering, and skiing. Route 40 passes through a tunnel directly underneath this slope.

The Reschen/Resia Pass, where the Italian and Austrian border officials control passports, is 1,934 feet (1,504 meters) above sea level. A major gateway to South Tyrol and more southerly provinces of Italy, the pass sees many thousands of Austrian, German, Swiss, French, Belgian, and Dutch tourists in summer and winter. The Reschen-Scheideck, a 4,774-foot (1,455-meter) ridge above the road, is the watershed between the Inn-Danube-Black Sea and the Adige-Adriatic river systems.

From the Reschen/Resia Pass, Austrian National Route 315 goes on to the ancient village of Nauders, where it is joined by Route 184 from the Swiss Engadin, and to the town of Landeck in the Inn Valley, 29 miles (47 kilometers) north of the frontier, on the main highway and railroad between the Austrian Tyrol and eastern Switzerland.

V.

GRAND
NORTH-SOUTH PASSAGE

❧

The Brenner Pass is one of Europe's principal north-south gateways and Italy's busiest border point. At 4,508 feet (1,375 meters) above sea level, it is relatively low as corridors across the Alps go and is open all year. Even after heavy snowstorms the Italian and Austrian traffic workers manage to clear the old Brenner Road, the new motorway, and the tracks of the Brenner railroad in a matter of hours.

Flagstones of an ancient Roman military road have been found on the pass; but people have crossed the flat saddle hundreds or, probably, thousands of years before the legions of Emperor Augustus did. The origin of the name *Brenner* is uncertain. According to one theory, it is derived from an Alpine tribe whom the ancient Romans called the Breoni. Another explanation is that in the fourteenth century the appellation of a farmstead, Brenner Hof, was transferred to the mountain passage. The German word *Brenner* means "burner," but also "brick maker" and "distiller" or "moonshiner."

Today the Brenner route is pounded mercilessly day and night by the behemoths of commercial transport; the cargo traffic has impressively increased since the founding of the European Community (now European Union) in 1958, and efforts to have a larger portion of the tonnage shipped by rail rather than on the road have so far had only limited success.

Most travelers who pass the Brenner nowadays are tourists—millions of them every year. Those coming from northern countries are proceeding to destinations not only in Italy, but also to Corsica, Greece, or North Africa, which they will reach by ferries. One of the numberless visitors to Italy who through the ages saw the Brenner is commemorated by a plaque on the Post Inn in the village of Brennero/Brenner: Johann Wolfgang von Goethe, who was a guest on September 9, 1786.

Another memorial, this one in the Brennero/Brenner station, honors Karl von Etzel, who built the railroad between 1863 and 1867. When it was opened it was considered a technical marvel. Unlike the other major trans-Alpine railroads, it crosses the main crest of the mighty mountains on the surface instead of through a tunnel.

I have passed the Brenner by train and car scores of times and once on foot during a hike and always wondered why such a beautiful country as Italy—the garden of Europe, home to immortal art and to a gifted, friendly people—maintains such a squalid entrance at the main crossing of its land frontiers. The Brennero/Brenner railroad station, on Italian territory, is drafty and inhospitable. Travelers in their coaches wait impatiently for the engines to be changed (the Austrian locomotive of the train is replaced by an Italian one, or vice versa) and the border guards to finish their passport and customs controls and to get moving again.

Brennero/Brenner Village, too, is Italian, and it isn't cheerful, either. The paint flakes off barracks and other buildings that went up under fascism to house soldiers, frontier guards, and railroad workers with their families. A couple of modest inns and several wine shops and the dense, dark forests on the heights of either side do little to brighten the morose scenery. When visiting, I always thought, Let's get out of this place. I pity the people who have to live in such sullen surroundings and breathe the exhaust fumes of countless cars and trucks that foul the chilly Alpine air; maybe the inhabitants have become inured to the road and rail noises all through their nights.

From the Brenner Pass the railroad tracks turn into the short Pflersch/Fleres Valley to descend almost 1,000 feet (300 meters) in a narrow loop through a spiraling tunnel and on comparatively steep gradients. At the time of its construction this section of the Brenner line was hailed as a triumph of railroad engineering. Looking out of the window when not in a tunnel, passengers get tantalizing glimpses of a quiet, green side valley, a paradise for trout fishers. The village of Pflersch/Fleres, a little above its railroad station (where few trains stop), was a gold-mining center in the Middle Ages. Today it is a starting point for mountaineers who want to take on the formidable Tribulaun massif, which is 10,158 feet (3,096 meters) high, covered with glaciers, and challenging even to experienced climbers because of its sheer walls and tumbling rocks.

The railroad line leaves the side valley at the former silver-mining and market village of Gossensass/Colle Isarco, until around 1960 a thriving resort. Today the once picturesque place seems suffocated by the massive concrete arches of the elevated Brenner motorway, A-22, which in less than 6 miles (9 kilometers) sweeps down straight from the Brenner Pass parallel to the young Eisack/Isarco River. The towering pillars of the motorway have spoiled the village's panorama. Gossensass/Colle Isarco, over-passed by the A-22 autostrada, also sees plenty of traffic on the old Brenner highway, which runs through the village. Motorists who use it save tolls.

Gossensass/Colle Isarco, at 3,602 feet (1,098 meters) altitude, with scarcely 1,000 permanent residents, has nearly one thousand guest beds in hotels, inns, and private homes, and many pleasant promenades in summer and ski lifts in winter. Yet the high-class clientele that once used to spend weeks in the village is no longer. Establishments with such pretentious names as Palace Hotel are only a memory.

❦

AUTUMN LOVE

One prominent guest during those mellow summers long before World War I was Henrik Ibsen. The Norwegian playwright had completed *The Wild Duck* in Gossensass in 1884 and on his return to the village in 1889 was honored by the mayor and the communal counselors, who had decided to name his old hillside lookout "Ibsen-Platz" (Ibsen Square).

There was an official parade, and Ibsen became short-winded when he had to march up the hill with the mayor and the village band in their traditional Tyrolean garb. I assume, although I have no authority to back me up on this, that the "Andreas Hofer Song" was played and chanted—it couldn't be missing from any Tyrolean celebration.

A concert was held beneath the just unveiled sign carrying the Norwegian's name. Afterward Ibsen found a chance to talk to a girl in the crowd; he had long noticed her in the dining room of his hotel, the Gröbner. (It was then a family-type place; it would later style itself Grand Hotel Gröbner.) The playwright was staying in Gossensass with his wife and their son Sigurd, who was in the diplomatic service. Mrs. Ibsen could not have been unaware of her husband's interest in the young woman, whom, during their meals they saw regularly at a neighboring table. The dramatist may have explained his roving eye with his need to store up impressions and material for his stage characters. His wife seems to have observed the prudent flirtation with amused tolerance. Soon the Norwegian, his wife, and their son would talk amiably with the girl.

She was Emilie Bardach of Vienna, eighteen years old— forty-three years Ibsen's junior. She and her family were spending the summer in Gossensass, and they must have been both flattered and puzzled by the famous fellow guest's attentions. It took some time before Ibsen was able to meet with Emilie alone, and there could have been some maneuvering by both to get rid of their relatives.

Sitting side by side on a bench near the "Ibsen-Platz" sign, they had a long conversation, which must have been at least as revealing as any dialogue in an Ibsen drama.

From Emilie's diary we know that after that talk she felt the sixty-one-year-old, seemingly cool Norwegian was actually a "volcano." Emilie somewhat complacently noted she had awakened "passions" in the playwright and described as "true love" what had started between them. During their talk, Ibsen appears to have fantasized aloud about divorcing his wife and living with the young Viennese. However, she reasonably reminded herself in the diary of "the obstacles, real life, the many years [of difference in their ages], the wife, the son."

Emilie read one of Ibsen's early works, *Love's Comedy*, in Gossensass. If he had given the volume to her, it was odd amorous strategy, because the verse play's bittersweet message is that romantic love, intense though it may be, can't last. Nor did the Gossensass idyll. The days in the mountain resort grew shorter, and in the evenings Emilie played the piano in the hotel, with her mature suitor a rapt listener. The end of summer was approaching.

Gossensass became windy and chilly, and the first snow flurries were reported from the Brenner Pass above the resort. Emilie's family decided it was time to return to Vienna; maybe they found the girl's friendship with the Norwegian celebrity had gone far enough. Before they left, Ibsen gave her a photo of himself with a dedication in German: "To the May sun of a September life—in Tyrol."

About a month later Ibsen wrote Emilie from Munich, then his home, that he had started a new work, but his imagination was wandering to "where it shouldn't." He continued: "I can't repress my memories of last summer. Nor do I want to. What I experienced I experience again and again—and ever again."

Ibsen and Emilie exchanged a few more letters, but at the end of 1890 he asked her to stop the correspondence for the time being. Emilie didn't know that the playwright had stayed on for a few days after her family's departure from Gossensass and had been approached by another young woman, a German. His new acquaintance must have been bolder, or pushier, than Emilie; she was a photographer from Munich. She and Ibsen saw each other in Munich afterward and appear to have become quite close.

Yet Ibsen didn't forget Emilie and Gossensass. Nearly nine years later when he was living again in Christiania (now Oslo), he sent her a new photo with a nostalgic dedication: "That summer in Gossensass was the happiest, most beautiful one in my entire life. I hardly dare think of it.—And yet I always must.—Always!" The portrait was his acknowledgment of a well-wishing telegram from Emilie on his seventieth birthday.

Gossensass/Colle Isarco too remembers Ibsen. It still has its Ibsen-Platz/Piazza Ibsen, and the village's tourist information office is located on it. Ask there for advice if you want to hike to Sterzing/Vipiteno and don't want to walk along the heavily trafficked highway. There are easy alternative paths.

৩৶

MEDIEVAL MINING

The upper valley of the Eisack/Isarco River, which rises near the Brenner Pass, is known as the Wipptal (there is no Italian name for it). It reaches from Gossensass/Colle Isarco to Franzensfeste/ Fortezza—some 20 miles (nearly 35 kilometers) of a tortuous stream between steep, wooded slopes and a few gloomy gorges, interrupted by the wide basin of Sterzing/Vipiteno (see chapter 1).

The town is little more than 3 miles (5 kilometers) south of Gossensass/Colle Isarco. The Renaissance core with its arcaded burghers' houses and the Town Hall is still intact. What's new in it is a Provincial Mining Museum at 20 Frundsberg-Strasse in a recently restored building known as the Jöchlsthurn (Jöchlsturm, or Jöchls' Tower). The complex, with terraced gables and an oriel, its windows secured with stout iron grills, is named after a long-extinct Jöchl family of mine operators; they must have made a lot of money, taken over a medieval defense tower, and expanded it with annexes and their own chapel. After the Jöchls died out, other members of the petty nobility lived in the building. In 1835 the Jöchlthurn became the courthouse, and when I first saw it the district court was still sitting in it.

The new museum, opened in the 1980s, documents the development of the mines in the environs of Sterzing and describes the town's relationship with that industry; various exhibits explain mining technology in the Middle Ages and the Renaissance.

116

Collections of minerals and old coins can be viewed on the museum's three levels. The large second-floor room containing the numismatics has a surprisingly beautiful carved-wood ceiling with the Jöchls' coat of arms in its midst. The museum is open mornings and afternoons Tuesday to Saturday from the beginning of April to the end of October.

Also relatively new in town is a World War II memorial near the old parish church, frescoed by a local artist. The panels on the monument show Sterzing men wearing steel helmets and heavy armament and marching in Hitler's army. It progressively shows the soldiers perishing in battle and the Angel of Death rising over the town's landmark Civic Tower as Allied aircraft carry out a bombing raid, ending with a Resurrection allegory.

A major portion of Hans Multscher's carved and painted altar, once in the parish church, is now on display in the new Multscher Museum in the old Deutschhaus (German House), a fifteenth-century building south of the churchyard that once was a headquarters of the Teutonic Knights; for many years it served as a hospital. The eight panels represent episodes from the life of the Virgin Mary, including an Annunciation and a Birth of Jesus, and scenes from Christ's Passion. The museum is open 10 A.M.–noon and 3–5 P.M. Monday to Saturday from the beginning of May to the end of October.

Though there are just a few recent architectural changes in the historic center of Sterzing/Vipiteno, someone who hasn't seen the town for three decades wouldn't recognize its outskirts. There, a jumble of service stations, fast-food places, wine shops, shoe stores, and tourist marts has proliferated since the A-22 was built. The autostrada exit closest to the Brenner Pass happens to be near Sterzing, and hundreds or even thousands of travelers every day make their first or last stop, as the case may be, on

Italian territory in the town. Cars, tourist coaches, and trucks park everywhere at the approaches to the old center, and business is thriving.

At the southern rim of the Sterzing basin, where the upper Eisack/Isarco Valley narrows again, two medieval strongholds occupy hilltops on either side of the river and the Brenner Road. During my first sojourn I walked up to both to take in the panorama. On the left, east of the Eisack, is the round Romanesque donjon of Sprechenstein Castle, surrounded by old walls. Reifenstein Castle, opposite, is more impressive. It rises on a rock above the charming hamlet of Elzenbaum; the word means "prune tree" in archaic Tyrolean, and the Italian name aptly chosen for it is Pruno. It has a quaintly old-fashioned inn.

Reifenstein Castle, which may be visited in conducted tours, was erected in the early twelfth century. For some time the castle was occupied by a chapter of the Teutonic Knights, and it eventually became one of the many properties of the immensely rich counts of Thurn and Taxis. The castle's Chapter Hall of the Teutonic Order is distinguished by late-Gothic wood carvings; a green hall is richly frescoed.

Several side valleys open into the Sterzing basin. The wide, green plain west of the town's parish church is formed by the confluence of various mountain streams. National Route 508 leads up to the Pennser Joch/Passo Pennes and goes on to Bolzano (page 73), and National Route 44 leads to the Jaufenpass/Passo del Giovo, proceeding to Merano (page 95). The quiet Ratschings/Racines and Ridnaun/Ridanna Valleys north of Route 44, with remote hamlets and long abandoned mines, are favorites of trekkers and, above all, skiers.

The narrow Pfitschtal/Val di Vizze east of Sterzing mounts for 20 miles (33 kilometers) to a pass on the Italian-Austrian border at an altitude of 7,385 feet (2,251 meters). I once tried to get there by car and soon wished I hadn't, because the winding road was very narrow for long stretches and a lot of jockeying was necessary whenever a vehicle came from the opposite direction. With a precipice on my left, I had to drive on for quite a while until I found a spot to turn around. The small villages and hamlets along the Pfitsch torrent don't see a great many tourists, but families with children spend very quiet summer vacations there, and mountain climbers use the valley's simple inns as base camps.

෯

An Elephant in
the Bishop's Town

Past the pilgrimage Church of Maria Trens, where my Maibad landlady, Luise, and her relatives once prayed before relaxing in the nearby inn's garden, the Brenner Road descends to the railroad and highway hub of Franzensfeste/Fortezza (the German name means "Francis's fortress" and the Italian name just "fortress"). Emperor Franz I of Austria in fact ordered a fort built on that strategic site in 1833; he died before it was completed, and it never served for any military operations.

The grim fortifications were meant to protect the Brenner route and the highway into the Pustertal/Val Pusteria (chapter 6), which branches off from there. Later Franzensfeste/Fortezza became a junction of the Brenner and Pustertal railroad lines; the tracks run right across the fort's outworks. A nearby artificial lake, created in 1940, supplies water for a power plant at Bressanone/Brixen.

Driving down the Brenner highway, National Route 12, another 5 miles (8 kilometers), the traveler notices on the left a large sign with the outline of an elephant and an arrow. It points the way to the Elefant Hotel, named after one of the most famous visitors of a city that has welcomed innumerable guests. The year was A.D. 1550, and an Indian elephant was trudging up the road to the Brenner Pass through the snowdrifts of December. The animal was a gift from King John III, the Fortunate, of Portugal to Emperor Ferdinand I; it had been shipped from Goa, then a Portuguese colony, and was being driven across the mountains in the manner in which Hannibal's African elephants passed the crest of the Maritime Alps nearly 1,800 years earlier.

In Brixen the pachyderm's handlers found it needed a break, and they let it rest for two weeks at the High Field Inn. The exotic traveler was a local sensation. Mountain farmers came down from their homesteads to gape at it together with the amazed townspeople. The inn's owner, postmaster Andrae Posch, at once changed his business's name to Inn at the Sign of the Elephant. He also commissioned a local artist, Lenhard Mair, to perpetuate the memorable event in painting. The fresco portraying the huge animal and its escort of turbaned Indians can still be seen on the street facade of the old wing of the Elefant Hotel, now a first-class establishment. The stoic jumbo from India did make it to the Brenner Pass and eventually to Innsbruck and Vienna, duly impressing the imperial court at its first appearance in late 1551; it would live in the emperor's menagerie another few years.

At the time of the elephant episode, the core of Brixen/ Bressanone, as it is represented in old pictures, looked essentially as it does today. The narrow, arcaded houses with their bow windows and decorative battlements on Grosse Lauben (Via Portici Maggiori), Kleine Lauben (Via Portici Minori), and the side alleys are from the fifteenth and sixteenth centuries. However, espresso bars, restaurants, and stores nestle today in the covered passageways as they do in Bolzano and Merano. Three stout gates of Brixen's medieval walls survive.

From the arcaded, pedestrians-only area it's just a few steps to an ecclesiastic complex with a cathedral, three other churches, a splendidly frecoed cloister, a seminary, and an imposing episcopal palace with walls and a moat.

Brixen has been the "Tyrolean Rome" since the early Middle Ages—a religious center in the Alps. Its long line of bishops once headed the Roman Catholic clergy in a vast mountain diocese, and between the eleventh century and 1803 were also temporal rulers as princes of the Holy Roman Empire, theoretically subject only to the emperor. Many of the bishops came from aristocratic families and some from the imperial House of Hapsburg.

The heads of the large Brixen diocese—like the prince-bishops of Trent farther south—did not administer their entire territory themselves. They entrusted vast chunks of it to local noblemen as episcopal bailiffs. As in feudal systems elsewhere and in other periods, the presumed vassals, who had their own castles and henchmen, soon acted as they liked, considered their func-tions hereditary, entered into alliances with other princes, and often conducted their own private wars.

One head of the Brixen diocese, a Bavarian named Poppo, became pope. He styled himself Damasus II but reigned for only twenty-three days, from July 17 to August 9, 1048, probably a victim of the "Roman fever" (malaria), which was for centuries virulent at the height of summer, if he wasn't a victim of some Roman poison plot.

Another bishop of Brixen, Nicolaus Cusanus or Nicholas of

Kues (1401–1464), the son of a wealthy boatsman and vintner on the Moselle River, was one of the most learned personages in the period of incipient humanism and the early Renaissance. A theologian, philosopher, mathematician, accomplished writer, and papal diplomat, he was an advocate of church reform and traveled widely—as far as Constantinople and the Netherlands—on ecclesiastical missions.

Pope Nicholas V gave him the red hat of a cardinal and in 1450 assigned him to the Tyrolean see, naming him also pontifical legate for all of Germany. The cathedral chapter of Brixen, the priestly body that was supposed to assist the bishop in the government of the cathedral and diocese, resented him as a meddlesome outsider, but he was able to impose a measure of discipline on the clergy.

Cusanus courted political trouble, however, when he sought to assert his authority over the independent-minded Benedictine nuns of the prestigious monastery of Sonnenburg in the nearby Pustertal, attempting to cloister them. The frisky nuns, all of them from aristocratic families, and their formidable abbess, Verena from Stuben in North Tyrol, resisted; they defied the bishop even when he and the pope inflicted severe church punishments on them. Duke Sigismund of Tyrol, whom we have encountered with his Scottish wife as inhabitant of the Princely Castle in Merano, chafed at the cardinal's moralizing—he himself kept a string of mistresses on the side—and rallied to the support of the stubborn nuns.

In the ensuing conflict, Cusanus was at one time taken prisoner, on other occasions repaired to some Alpine stronghold, and eventually abandoned his diocese. Virtually a refugee, he died near Rome fourteen years after being installed as prince-bishop of Brixen. His tomb is in his titular church as a cardinal, San

Pietro in Vincoli near the Colosseum in Rome, where fifty years later Michelangelo's statue of Moses would be placed.

Today Brixen's Cathedral Square still conveys a sense of clerical power, but the bishops no longer reside in the city since their official move to Bolzano in 1964. The square's east side is dominated by a twin-towered edifice in triumphant Baroque style, erected at the middle of the eighteenth century on the site of a medieval basilica. The two towers of the cathedral are much older than the bulk of the church, showing Renaissance elements in their upper windows.

To the left of the cathedral is Brixen's late-Gothic parish church from the end of the fifteenth century, with a tall, whitish tower crowned by a needle-shaped roof. An arcaded courtyard between the two buildings contains tombstones bearing reliefs of imperious- or pious-looking prelates of past centuries, as well as the city's war memorials.

The right (south) side of the cathedral is adjoined by a famous cloister with frescoes from the fourteenth and fifteenth centuries that have recently been restored. The paintings on the walls and vaults are by various local artists whose identity is a matter of conjecture and date from various times—whenever a churchman or some other patron commissioned a panel. The murals therefore do not constitute a thematic cycle; instead they present random scenes from the Hebrew Bible and the Gospels—Adam and Eve, Moses, Job, the Madonna, the Passion of Jesus, the Apostles— and from church history. The cloister, around a garden with shrubbery, provides access to the former private chapel of the bishops and to a small baptismal church.

Between the cathedral and the Eisack/Isarco River is the seminary, which prepares students for the priesthood. The building, from the second half of the eighteenth century, is in late-

Baroque style, with a large courtyard and a frescoed church of its own.

◈

DARK HOST

On the north side of Cathedral Square is the Town Hall, with a crenellated front. Two cafes and old burghers' houses look out on the square and its pond, fountain, and flower beds. On festive occasions the civic band offers outdoor concerts in front of the cathedral.

Nearby, on the narrow Domgasse (Cathedral Lane), is an old tavern where members of the cathedral chapter and lay officials of the episcopal bureaucracy once used to relax. The place is known as the Finsterwirt, or Dark Host, because it seems patrons could get something to eat and drink even after the start of the curfew that the prince-bishop (maybe no other than stern Cardinal Cusanus) had imposed, as long as no candle or torch was lit. Thoroughly modernized in its interior, Dark Host is still in business, though with plenty of light.

The former episcopal residence, a four-hundred-year-old Renaissance palace with the remnants of a moat and walls, a short walk to the southwest of Cathedral Square, is now a museum. The magnificent courtyard with a double loggia over ground-floor arcades is adorned with twenty-four statues in second-story niches, representing members of the House of Hapsburg. The first-floor rooms contain ten thousand figurines, a collection of three centuries' worth of crèches, plastic representations of the Nativity. The former staterooms of the prince-bishops and the Diocesan Museum, displaying wood carvings, sculptures, paintings, and liturgical objects, can be visited on two upper floors. The palace gardens are now a lovingly nursed public park with a profusion of flowers.

There are much greenery and many banks of flowers in and around Brixen/Bressanone; esplanades along the Eisack/Isarco River invite strollers and joggers. The city, situated 1,834 feet (559 meters) above sea level and surrounded by high mountains, has a dry, sunny, and relatively mild climate. During the Victorian era, Brixen was a resort where well-heeled people with pulmonary ailments would sojourn. At present Brixen/Bressanone teems on school days with students from nearby towns and villages who attend one of the city's several educational institutions, as well as shoppers from the surroundings and transient tourists. In the evenings and especially on weekends the city, which is home to seventeen thousand people, looks sleepy.

To Italians in faraway parts of the nation, the name *Bressanone* instead conjures up the image of a fashionable place for slimming, eating healthy food, getting plenty of exercise, and undergoing hydrotherapy and other treatments.

An establishment for doing all these things is the Sanatorium Dr. von Guggenberg, in a park on the city's southeastern outskirts near the confluence of the Rienza and Eisack/Isarco Rivers. It is the oldest and one of the most prestigious of Italy's many health farms. The sanatorium was founded in 1890 by a physician, Otto von Guggenberg, who had long worked with the Reverend Sebastian Kneipp (1820–1897), a Bavarian priest who advocated "natural" lifestyles and the copious use of water to treat a vast range of diseases. The "Kneipp cures" won many followers all over central Europe, and many people still practice them. Four generations of Guggenbergs have run the sanatorium for more than a hundred years, always faithful to the Kneipp procedures.

Wine lovers trek or drive along the east bank of the Eisack/ Isarco upstream for 2 miles (about 3 kilometers) to sample the vintages of the Augustinian canons at Neustift/Novacella and possibly take a few bottles with them. The canons' monastery is eight hundred years old, a cluster of buildings from various epochs surrounded by vineyards and gardens. Coming from the north, it is indeed near Brixen that the traveler will see the first vineyards south of the Brenner Pass.

Neustift/Novacella operates not only a winery, but also a boarding school and is known for a sumptuous library with rich stucco decorations and an internal gallery, as well as for its curious Chapel of St. Michael. This little circular structure from the fifteenth century looks like a scale model of Castel Sant'Angelo near the Vatican—the medieval papal fortress on the Tiber built over the tomb of Emperor Hadrian—and is called the Engelsburg, or Angel's Castle. It is a fitting landmark for the "Tyrolean Rome."

I have visited Brixen/Bressanone at least thirty times in my life, spent weeks in the city on occasion, and thought I knew everything about it that is worth knowing. But I didn't. Recently I struck up a conversation with a genial Nigerian in the breakfast room of the more-than-one-hundred-year-old Jarolim Hotel. Was he on vacation? I asked. "Oh no," he replied. "I'm buying special optical instruments that are being made here." I had never noticed any high-tech plant in the city. Yet, sure enough, a young English-speaking Tyrolean in a business suit arrived presently to take the customer to the industrial zone of Brixen/Bressanone.

I had always driven past this agglomeration of low, modern buildings on the southern approaches to the city without paying much attention to it. When I at last explored it, I found a collection of small and medium-size industries ranging from a state-of-the-art dairy and other food-processing enterprises to the metal-working and optical firm that was also selling its products to West Africa.

When Michel de Montaigne traveled to Italy in 1580, he was struck in Brixen by hamlets, entire villages, and belfries all the way to high altitudes on the mountains surrounding the city, and he remarked in his *Journal* that it seemed mysterious how people could get up there. The panorama of the mountain villages with their church steeples is at present still one of the charms of Brixen/Bressanone, but instead of climbing up and down on arduous tracks, their inhabitants now ride motor scooters and cars on paved roads.

The city's "house mountain" is the 8,215-foot (2,504-meter) Plose near the east bank of the Eisack/Isarco. A road and a funicular rise to spots near the summit of this year-round recreation area, and chair lifts take tourists and skiers farther up. The views from the Plose embrace the Etsch/Adige Valley, the glaciers and highest peaks of the Tyrolean Alps in the north, and the Dolomites to the southeast.

ॐ

HOLY MOUNTAIN

South of the industrial district of Brixen/Bressanone the valley narrows again, cliffs advancing on the western side of the highway. On the opposite (left) side is a turnoff into a secluded side valley, named after its main town, Villnöss (Italian: Val di Funes). The provincial road, running for some 10 miles (16 kilometers) along a torrent, has no eastern exit and ends in unpaved tracks and steep paths. Without through traffic, the Villnöss/Funes Valley has until now remained comparatively pristine, although it has lately attracted an increasing number of Alpine purists for summer or skiing vacations.

Village, farm, and field names are mostly Ladin; Villnöss itself may be a corruption of *villes nöes* (new houses). Local people at present speak Tyrolean German. There is archaeological evidence that this remote corner of South Tyrol was inhabited in prehistoric times; ancient Roman coins have come to light there, too.

The visitor coming from the Brenner Road who turns into the provincial highway first passes a gorge near the picturesque hamlet of Gufidaun below the uninhabited Sommersberg Castle. After the village of Pardell the valley gets broader, disclosing a friendly, untarnished landscape of green fields and pastures near the stream, isolated farmhouses on the slopes, dense forests higher up, and to the south the giant gray Dolomite prongs of the Gaislerspitzen/Le Odle (the Ladin name means "the Needles"), which soar to nearly 10,000 feet (more than 3,000 meters) altitude.

The center of the valley is the twin town of St. Peter and Villnöss (San Pietro-Funes), with a couple of good hotels and several inns. Toward the upper end of the valley, surrounded by fields and grassland, is the eye-catching solitary little Church of St. Johann, with its onion-roofed steeple.

On a forested slope above the last village in the valley, St. Magdalena, stands an isolated rock, about fifteen feet (three meters) high. A plaque identifies it as the "Lutheran Church," stating that in the time of the Roman Catholic Counter-Reformation "supporters of the new doctrine" used to gather in a nearby cave. The religious dissidents who held clandestine meetings there weren't actually Lutherans, but Anabaptists, followers of the radical Christian sect that advocated complete separation between church and state and rebaptism for believers. The leader of the

Tyrolean Anabaptists, Jakob Huter, was captured in the sexton's house in the hamlet of Gufidaun near the mouth of the Villnöss Valley, where he was hiding in 1535, and burned at the stake as a heretic the year afterward in Innsbruck.

Back on the Brenner highway, Route 12, soon after the Villnöss/Funes turnoff the traveler reaches a highway junction with connections to the Klausen/Chiusa exit of the Brenner motorway, A-22, and to National Route 242 into the Val Gardena and Ladinia (see chapter 7).

Approaching Klausen/Chiusa, visitors realize why the German and Italian names of the town imply closure: it is tightly squeezed between the rocky mountains and the river. The town's coat of arms significantly displays a key—the Brenner route could easily be shut here.

Klausen/Chiusa huddles at the foot of a steep rock, 637 feet (194 meters) high. On top of the rock is the Benedictine nunnery of Sabiona/Säben. I have been told repeatedly by local people that a young nun once jumped out of a window of her cell to her death deep below, but I was never able to find out when the tragedy was supposed to have happened or whether it is just a Tyrolean popular legend, like King Laurin, only more morbid.

Archaeological finds prove that the rock above Klausen/Chiusa was inhabited in the Bronze Age. Excavations since the 1970s have also furnished evidence of Christian houses of worship existing there since the fifth century. To devout Tyroleans Sabiona/Säben is their "holy mountain," one of the region's earliest centers of Christian missionary efforts. A bishop is assumed to have resided on the rock as early as the sixth century. Around A.D. 1000 the bishops of Sabiona transferred their see to Brixen, but the hill above Klausen/Chiusa remained an important religious site. The heads of the Brixen diocese maintained a fortified residence there, which was later taken over by noblemen and in 1535 was destroyed by fire. In the late seventeenth century the Benedictine nuns transformed the ruin into a monastery, which later was repeatedly enlarged.

A steep path leads from Klausen's Town Hall up the rock past the thirteenth-century Branzoll Castle. Depending on how rapidly you climb, you will reach the summit in thirty to forty-five minutes. I knew a woman in Klausen/Chiusa who used to walk up the hill daily to attend mass.

The monastery cannot be visited because the about two dozen nuns now living in it are strictly cloistered; their voices can be heard in their Church of Our Lady when they sing their office at certain canonical hours, unseen by the congregation. The church, a Baroque edifice built in 1652, is accessible.

More interesting than the nuns' church is the Church of the Holy Cross at the highest point of the rock, which is one of the region's oldest ecclesiastic structures, erected over even earlier churches. An unidentified Italian or Italian-inspired artist decorated its interior during the seventeenth century with frescoes that were intended to create an illusion of colonnaded halls and architectural depth as a framework for biblical scenes.

The rock of Sabiona commands a fine panorama of the Ei-sack/Isarco Valley, but the view is more impressive from below because of the steepness of the rock walls. Among those whom it struck was Albrecht Dürer. The Nuremberg draftsman, engraver, and painter sketched various Alpine landscapes during his first journey to Italy in 1494. He may have spent a night in Klausen, for he made at least one drawing of the fortified hill, and he used the Klausen panorama as a realistic background in his famous engraving *Nemesis* (also known as the *Great Fortuna*, circa 1503), which portrays the allegorical figure of a winged goddess balancing on a revolving sphere.

On Klausen's river promenade stands a bronze statue of Father Joachim Haspinger (1776–1858), a monk in the still existing Capuchin convent at the southern outskirts of the town, who was an aide to the Tyrolean hero Andreas Hofer in the uprising against the Bavarians and the French in 1809.

Waidbruck/Ponte Gardena, less than 4 miles (6 kilometers) south of Klausen/Chiusa, provides the main entrance to the Gherdëina/Gröden Valley (chapter 7). Some scholars insist that Waidbruck/Ponte Gardena is the birthplace of Walther von der Vogelweide. Others disagree, claiming that Lower Austria or southern Germany deserves this recognition. The nearby village of Barbian on the west bank of the Eisack/Isarco is on the spot where the old Roman road from Bolzano across the Ritten/Renon high plateau joined the present Brenner route.

I recommend a hike from Barbian up the slope at least as far as the charming hamlet of Bad Dreikirchen/Tre Chiese (Three Churches), which is reached by a path across the forest in about an hour. Three chapels from the thirteenth to the fifteenth centuries, each with a short, square turret, cling to one another there; why they were built so closely together is unexplained. Patches of frescoes are visible on the outsides of the three barnlike mini-churches and on interior walls. One of the trio, St. Magdalene's, has a fine late-Gothic altarpiece representing the coronation of the Virgin Mary.

Cows graze on the rising green tracts nearby. There are a few houses whose inhabitants are all somehow related to one another, an old inn, and an outdoor swimming pool. A cold alkaline-saline spring is nearby, prompting the hamlet to proudly call itself a "bath" or spa. The views of the emerald Eisack/ Isarco Valley deep below are astounding—villages, hamlets, and scattered church steeples, wooded mountains across the river with their farmsteads, and immense Dolomite peaks.

Bad Dreikirchen/Tre Chiese, at 3,675 feet (1,120 meters) altitude, is an enchanted spot, blessedly untouched by the motor age and mass tourism. For trekkers, footpaths lead up to the Rittnerhorn (page 72) and to the Ritten/Renon. The Ritten road that the ancient Romans had built became obsolete when a fourteenth-century contractor, Heinrich Kunter, won permission to create a highway across the porphyry gorges of the lower Eisack River and collect tolls from users. Today's National Route 12 essentially follows Kunter's rocky corridor south of Barbian, whereas the engineers of the new Brenner motorway tunneled through mountain spurs and strung viaducts across ravines to avoid curves.

Approaching Bolzano on Route 12, one passes a steep turnoff to the Schlern/Sciliar massif (page 175), which Bolzano people like to visit on weekends, at the village of Blumau/Prato all'Isarco on the river's left bank. Another turnoff southward, a few miles farther, leads to the Great Dolomite Road (page 182). A branch of Route 12 and the Brenner autostrada, A-22, bypass the region's capital on its southern outskirts to proceed straight to the lower Etsch/Adige Valley.

১৯

ON THE WINE ROAD

In order to see South Tyrol's sun-graced Wine Road with its vineyards, castles, mansions, inns, and wineries, travelers must leave the Brenner highway, Route 12, or Motorway A-22, cross the Talvera/Talfer River into Bolzano's left-bank Gries section, and take the long, straight Viale Druso to Eppan/Appiano. This is a group of two dozen villages and hamlets on a rolling plateau between the Etsch/Adige and the steep ridges to its east. The area is often very hot in summer; the best times for a visit are in May and, especially, in autumn after the grape harvest.

The Castle of Hocheppan (High Eppan), crowning a porphyry rock at an altitude of 2,087 feet (636 meters), dominates the landscape and offers a panorama stretching from the upper Etsch/Adige Valley and Merano on the left to the city of Bolzano with its Rose Garden backdrop straight ahead, and to the lower reaches of the river and Salurn/Salorno on the right. The ruin, from the twelfth century, was once the residence of the counts of Eppan, who for generations were political rivals of the counts of Tyrol but who eventually lost out to them and their allies.

A visit to the once mighty stronghold requires some climbing on a footpath from a spot above the village of Missian. The walk is worthwhile not only for the vistas, but also for famous early-thirteenth-century frescoes in the castle's chapel, close to a precipice. Access to the chapel is from the castle's inner courtyard. A faded mural on the outside shows a deer hunt; the paintings in the interior picture Jesus, the Madonna, Apostles, and other biblical figures. The chapel's decorations, probably executed by more than one painter, appear influenced by Byzantine art. Hocheppan is a quiet place where one may pleasantly spend a couple of hours; refreshments are available.

The center of the Eppan/Appiano cluster is the village of St. Michael, with several hotels, pensions, and Renaissance houses that look urban rather than rural, attesting to old wealth. From St. Michael, National Route 42 winds in many bends up to the

Mendel Pass/Passo della Mendola, 4,472 feet (1,363 meters) above sea level, a wooded saddle with hotels on the administrative border between the autonomous provinces of Bolzano/Südtirol and Trento. It is cool on the pass even on hot August days, and the panorama, with the Dolomites to the northeast, is grand. The western slope of the ridge, descending into the valley of the Noce River/Val di Non, is less precipitous than its eastern flank from St. Michael to the Mendel/Mendola Pass.

The signposted Wine Road runs north to south, roughly parallel to the Brenner motorway and the Brenner highway. It is nearly 24 miles (38 kilometers) long and links seven towns and villages on the west bank of the Etsch/Adige River, comprising 7,800 acres (3,200 hectares) of vineyards, nine times the area of Central Park in Manhattan.

Driving on the Wine Road southward from the Eppan/Appiano villages, one arrives quickly at the vintners' capital, Kaltern/Caldaro, at 1,332 feet (406 meters) altitude. Parked tourist coaches, particularly in spring and autumn, indicate that the old market town with its various church towers is an Eden for wine lovers. The town square, ennobled by a Baroque fountain and Renaissance houses, is surmounted by the mighty, isolated belfry of the parish church. A cableway from Kaltern/Caldaro goes up to the Mendel/Mendola Pass.

Higher sections of the town and the slopes above it command a pretty view of the Kalterersee/Lago di Caldaro, a lake less than 2 miles (3 kilometers) to the south, as well as of the vineyards and a forested hill framing it. "Kalterersee" has long become a trade name under which light red wines from South Tyrol are being marketed all over Europe, although only a small fraction of them can actually have been grown around the lake, which is only 1.25 miles (2 kilometers) long and less than 1 mile (1.5

kilometers) wide at its broadest part. At any rate, the aficionados filling the many taverns, restaurants, and inns at Kaltern/Caldaro and around the lake seem to hope that the real thing is being poured for them.

Kaltern/Caldaro fittingly boasts a South Tyrolean Wine Museum. It was created in 1955 in the Ringberg Castle near the lake and in the late 1980s was moved to its present seat, a former winery at the town center, 1 Goldgasse, off the main square. It is open 9 A.M.–noon and 2–6 P.M. Tuesday to Saturday, 10 A.M.–noon Sunday, from Easter to the end of October.

The vaulted showrooms tell the history of local winegrowing from antiquity to the present. Displays include old vintners' and coopers' tools; huge wine presses; vats and barrels in an authentic former wine cellar; ancient tavern signs; and drinking vessels of wood, copper, and glass. There is also the model of a nineteenth-century vineyard guardian with a costume meant to frighten off grape thieves; from the dummy's fantastic feather cap dangle the carcasses of animals and other weird objects, making the wearer appear like a shaman.

Following the Wine Road south of the Kaltern/Caldaro lake, one comes in a few miles to the village of Tramin/Tremeno. It has lent its name to the internationally popular gewürztraminer table wines; today almost all of them are grown in distant France. Tramin's village core, with its tall Gothic church tower, is surrounded by scores of hotels and wine taverns. The Wine Road ends at Kurtatsch/Cortaccia and a string of smaller villages and hamlets near Salurn/Salorno.

Travelers hastening to southern destinations bypass the Wine Road to reach Salurn/Salorno by rail, on the Brenner highway, or on the Brenner motorway along the broad, canalized Etsch/Adige east of the vintners' plateau. The old vineyards in the fertile, flat, and sunny valley tend to shrink as they are being increasingly converted into fruit plantations, which are more profitable at present. Agribusiness has above all favored apple-growing lately.

The old Brenner highway passes the town of Auer/Ora, with a turnoff to National Route 48, which leads into the Val di Fiemme of Trento Province and the Great Dolomite Road (page 182). Next, along the Brenner Road, Route 12, is Neumarkt/Egna. The little town's German name means "new market"— it was rebuilt after a catastrophic fire in 1331; at its center, with its arcaded main street, however, the "new" place looks ancient enough. One of the oldest houses, 24 Andreas-Hofer-Strasse, is since 1990 the seat of a Museum for Everyday Culture. On display under wooden beams in the renovated building are objects used in middle-class households between circa 1850 and 1950, such as kitchen utensils, crockery, spinning wheels, mousetraps, toys, and toiletry items. The collection was assembled privately and is being continually enlarged by a local group. The museum is open 4–6 P.M. Tuesday to Friday, 10 A.M.–noon on Sunday, from April to November.

The village of Salurn/Salorno south of Neumarkt/Egna and some 20 miles (32 kilometers) south of Bolzano used to be the southernmost German-speaking settlement in the district, but the village center has today clearly an Italian character. Tyrolean is still heard in the nearby hamlets and farmhouses.

Towering limestone walls and cliffs advance toward the Etsch/Adige River from both sides as in a huge stage set, forming a gorge that through the millennia has had strategic importance and therefore saw much fighting. A rock resembling a giant rotten tooth above Salurn/Salorno is believed to have been a stronghold already of Rhaetian tribes before the Romans subdued them; it carries the bleak ruins of a keep and castle walls from the eleventh or twelfth century.

The official border between the autonomous provinces of Bolzano/Südtirol and Trento runs south of Salurn/Salorno. The street signs and other inscriptions are no longer bilingual; flat-roofed buildings, many of them new, multiply; the entire scenery becomes distinctly Italian.

The ancient city of Trent (Italian: Trento) is now ringed with modern suburbs, ugly high-rise buildings in clusters, and industrial parks. The well-maintained urban core with its magnificent Romanesque-Gothic cathedral and Renaissance palaces is an architectural treasure.

Venice, only a couple of hours by car and three hours by train, at times seems even closer, judging by the Trentino idiom, art, and cuisine. Yet visitors will also find many specifically Alpine traits and treats in the province and its capital. The valleys and mountains of the Trentino are studded with the castles of former aristocratic clans bearing names like Arco, Castelbarco, Cles, Lodron, and Thun, which recur in the political, ecclesiastical, and cultural history of central Europe.

VI.

THREE
TYROLS

❧

The Val Pusteria/Pustertal Express departs from Innsbruck's central railroad station toward noon every day, crosses the Austrian-Italian frontier twice, and arrives around three P.M. in the city of Lienz, which looks out on jagged Dolomite peaks. During the trip the train never leaves the historic region of Tyrol, and the traveler sees a cross section of the three parts into which it is today divided—North Tyrol, South Tyrol, and East Tyrol.

Many Tyroleans speak also of a fourth section, which they call Welschtirol (Italian Tyrol), meaning the present autonomous province of Trento. The Italian-speaking Trentino (Trento Province) indeed belonged to the Crown Land Tyrol of Austria-Hungary until 1918, yet the majority of its inhabitants today consider themselves good Italians. A political movement exists nevertheless that calls itself the Trentino-Tyrolean Autonomist Party, and it has lately been gaining strength, as evidenced in election returns.

North and south of the Brenner there is, at any rate, a diffuse sentiment of regional identity and separateness from other Austrians and other Italians, much the way the Quebecois in Canada, the Welsh in Britain, the Bretons in France, the Catalans in Spain, and the Flemish people in Belgium feel.

In few places on the sunny side of the Alps are pan-Tyrolean attitudes as strong as they are in the Pustertal, the longest east-west passage in that area. The valley is really two rivers flowing in opposite directions: the Rienza, which falls into the Eisack/Isarco at Brixen, and the Drava, a tributary of the Danube. A broad saddle, 3,989 feet (1,214 meters) high, near the town of Toblach/Dobbiaco is the watershed between the two fluvial systems delivering water to the Adriatic and Black Seas and represents a link rather than a partition between the two parts of the valley.

About 40 miles (65 kilometers) of the Pustertal are on Italian territory, a broad, densely wooded corridor that at every bend discloses new, attractive vistas. The valley provides relatively easy access to the Dolomites and their main center, Cortina d'Ampezzo. The side valleys of the Pustertal, some of which are Ladin-speaking, offer impressive scenery and rise toward steep slopes, extended glaciers, and high peaks, attracting climbers and skiers. The Val Pusteria/Pustertal Express, despite its breezy name, becomes a local train when it reaches the long valley, halting at most of the many railroad stops. It is a far cry from the legendary Riviera Express, which was composed entirely of deluxe sleepers and diners of the International Sleeping Car Company. At the apex of the belle époque, before World War I, the Riviera Express rolled through the valley three times a week without stopping on its way from Budapest and Vienna to Cannes on the French Riviera and back.

Driving a car in the Pustertal at the height of the summer or winter tourist season can be a frustrating experience because National Route 49, which runs its whole length, is in some sections narrow and battered and has many curves. Yet many local people have stubbornly resisted projects to build a motorway in their valley on the ground that such an autostrada would detract from its environment.

The climate of the green Pustertal is a little less balmy than are the other major valleys on the south side of the Alps. Vineyards are lacking, while tall pines, spruces, firs, and other kinds of evergreen trees prevail in the forests that cover many slopes. In the hamlets and solitary farmhouses the old Tyrolean folkways are still alive. Natives who visit other parts of the region will proudly stress that they are "Pusterer," a badge of Tyrolean authenticity.

The root of the name *Puster* is controversial; one explanation is that the word is derived from the Slavic *bistrica*, meaning "bright river." Slovenians, a Slavic people, have indeed migrated up the Drava Valley for hundreds of years and settled here and there in Carinthia and in East and South Tyrol.

୬୧

A PITCHFORK JEANNE D'ARC

The western entrance to the Pustertal is from Franzensfeste/ Fortezza by rail and highway and from Brixen/Bressanone by National Route 49. The first villages along the Rienza River that the traveler sees are unpretentious summer vacation spots, each with a few inns and hotels. A path from the market town Mühlbach/Rio di Pusteria leads in about an hour's walk to the village of Spinges/Spinga, at 3,612 feet (949 meters) altitude, which has a fine panorama.

The out-of-the-way village is hallowed ground to patriotic Tyroleans because of the valor shown by the "Maid of Spinges" in 1797. She was Catarina Lanz, a farm servant of Ladin descent who joined the local peasants to fight French revolutionary troops that were on their way to meet General Bonaparte. With her pitchfork Catarina helped the farmers' force defeat the invaders. We shall encounter a statue of this Tyrolean Jeanne d'Arc, complete with pitchfork, in the Ladin valleys (page 181).

Vintl/Vandoies and the villages farther east along Route 49 all have their habitués who return year after year to stay a few weeks in simple inns, swim in the pools, walk a lot, explore the small side valleys, or do some skiing.

St. Lorenzen/San Lorenzo di Sebato, nearly 20 miles (32 kilometers) east of Franzensfeste/Fortezza, is near a gorge that forms the mouth of one of the Ladin valleys: the Gadertal/Abtei Tal/Val Badia. On a rocky hill at the opposite (north) side of the Rienza River once rose the castlelike Sonnenburg Monastery, whose irrepressible Abbess Verena and her aristocratic Benedictine nuns flouted the austere rules that Cardinal Nicolaus Cusanus tried to impose on them more than five hundred years ago (page 122).

Boccaccio would have found the ambiance at the "Sun Castle" convent congenial with his mocking tastes. As in other religious houses favored by noble ladies in the mellow autumn of the Middle Ages, the nuns thoroughly enjoyed their communal life. Lay sisters and male stewards were at their service; they occasionally journeyed to weddings of relatives or friends and other celebrations; and gossip about romantic intrigues was not infrequent. Once in a while a nun would run off to get married. Small wonder that the reverend mothers of Sonnenburg didn't care for getting cloistered by the zealous bishop of Brixen.

Then the Protestant Reformation and the Roman Catholic Counter-Reformation came, and new moral rigor arrived also at the Sonnenburg convent. Yet in 1785 Emperor Joseph II, the enlightened authoritarian, closed the nunnery in the Pustertal along with many other such institutions throughout Austria because he disapproved of religious communities that were not active in teaching, nursing, or other work he considered useful for the state. The Sonnenburg complex was sold, and it eventually decayed. Today only the abbess's wing still stands; it has become a thirty-two-room hotel with the name of the old monastery.

From St. Lorenzen it's only 2.5 miles (4 kilometers) to Bruneck/Brunico, the main town of the Pustertal. It is named after a Bishop Bruno von Kirchberg of Brixen, who founded it in the middle of the thirteenth century; the word *Bruneck* means "Bruno's corner," and the correct pronunciation of the Italian name *Brunico* is with the stress on the first syllable. Prettily situated in a hollow opposite the entrance to the Taufers/Tures side valley, the town is spreading below a wooded hill with a castle that the bishops of Brixen used as a summer residence. Today Bruneck with its outlying sections has fifteen thousand residents.

The historic part of the town lies on the left (south) bank of the Rienza and centers on the curving main street, Stadtgasse, which is lined with battlemented old buildings. The walls, with four gates, that enclose old Bruneck connect with the fortifications of the castle. The former episcopal summer residence is now the seat of an international academy that conducts art classes in summer.

The parish church, its two towers surmounted by pointed roofs, was rebuilt around the middle of the nineteenth century; it has a sixteenth-century choir and contains a cross with a life-size statue of the crucified Christ that is attributed to Michael Pacher, but which may actually be the work of one of his disciples. Pacher (circa 1435–1498), among the greatest artists produced by South Tyrol, was a native of Bruneck and member of a talented family of wood-carvers and painters. An inscription at 29 Stadtgasse records that he had his workshop there.

On a slope southwest of the old city is an evergreen-shaded World War I cemetery with eight hundred graves of Austrian, German, Italian, and Russian soldiers.

The Taufer/Tures Valley, opening north of Bruneck, and its side valleys are highly picturesque, bordered with dark forests, the slopes studded with mountain farms in arduous locations up to 4,800 feet (about 1,450 meters) above sea level. An electric railroad that once ran from Bruneck/Brunico for 10.5 miles (17 kilometers) to Sand in Taufers/Campo Tures has long been replaced by bus service.

❧

An American's Blisters

The smiling village of Gais (for once the Tyrolean and Italian names are the same), at an altitude of 2,759 feet (841 meters), not quite 4 miles (6 kilometers) north of Bruneck, was important in the life of Ezra Pound (see pages 89–91) and is mentioned in his *Pisan Cantos* (LXXVII). Pound, leading a compartmentalized existence, shuttled for decades between his wife and his mistress, the American expatriate violinist Olga Rudge. The poet was living in Rapallo on the Italian Riviera in 1925 when Olga gave birth to their daughter, Mary, at Bressanone/Brixen. The newborn was entrusted to a Gais farmer's wife, Johanna Marcher, who at the time happened to be at the Bressanone hospital and had just lost a baby.

In her memoir *Discretions* (Little, Brown, New York, 1971), Mary de Rachewiltz, Pound's daughter, tells how she was brought up in Gais like a little Tyrolean girl, exclusively speaking the Pusterer dialect, tending sheep, doing other farmwork, and occasionally receiving puzzling visits by "the lady" and "the gentleman"—her biological parents. Because of the language barrier, her grandfather, Homer Pound, could not communicate with Mary, then four years old, when he visited her at the Gais farm in 1929. Soon afterward, Mary saw her mother's home in Venice for the first time but was happy to return to her foster parents' farm.

Mary was later sent by her real parents to an exclusive boarding school in Florence, where she improved her elementary-school Italian, learned English, and stayed with her father and mother in Rapallo. She eventually went back to Gais. After the fall of Mussolini in 1943, Pound, who was then in Rome and almost penniless, hitchhiked and for long stretches walked all the way to Gais in the hope of finding asylum there. When he arrived in the farmhouse that was his daughter's home, he was exhausted, with blistered feet and swollen ankles. That night he told Mary for the first time that he had a wife and a son.

Pound was detained by United States authorities when the Allied troops occupied northern Italy. His daughter worked for some time as the village secretary in Gais and as a nurse in a Cortina d'Ampezzo hospital. She married Boris de Rachewiltz, and they went to live in the ruined thirteenth-century Neuhaus Castle once inhabited by local barons, on a mountain above Gais. The couple later moved to the Brunnenburg near Merano, and Neuhaus Castle is today an inn.

Visitors now find plenty of accommodations in the Taufer/ Tures Valley and along the streams that flow into it. The area, with its steep grassland, thick forests, torrents, waterfalls, and mountain farms below the glaciers and lofty summits, has become popular with summer vacationers and skiers.

The valley's main center is Sand in Taufers, also called just Taufers or, in Italian, Campo Tures, at 2,844 feet (867 meters) altitude at the confluence of the Ahrn and Reinbach torrents. On a rocky hill, a little to the village's north, stands the impressive Taufers Castle, a complex from the thirteenth century that was repeatedly altered and enlarged since then and restored in 1907. The wood paneling in its many rooms and halls is in part very old, and some carved ceilings are from the Renaissance. Frescoes in an upstairs chapel are by an artist of the Pacher workshop in Bruneck, circa 1480. The castle, which is privately owned, may be visited in guided tours daily during the main tourist seasons and on Sunday and some weekdays during the remainder of the year.

The upper part of the Taufers/Tures Valley, north of Sand, is a severely beautiful gorge, called the Ahrntal/Valle Aurina. Copper was mined in its mountains for hundreds of years until the second half of the nineteenth century, especially above the village of Steinhaus/Cà di Pietra. A mining museum is to be created in a four-story mine company house that the municipality bought and restored in the early 1990s.

A little church for copper miners on a mountainside known as Heiligengeist (Holy Spirit), at 5,312 feet (1,619 meters) above sea level near the hamlet of Kasern/Casere at the end of the valley, was consecrated by Nicolaus Cusanus soon after he became bishop of Brixen/Bressanone in 1450.

The Ahrn/Aurina Valley, with its forbidding rock walls, is a magnet for experienced Alpinists. One of them was Count Tolomei, the Italian nationalist (page 11) who in 1904 from there scaled a 9,550-foot (2,911-meter) peak that was then known as the Glockenkarkopf. On the summit he carved a large letter *I* into the rock to signify that the peak on the watershed between the river system flowing toward the Adriatic, the Danube, and eventually the Black Sea should be Italian, though it was then deep in Austria-Hungary. After World War I the Allied framers of the peace treaties awarded the mountain to Italy. Now officially called by the name Tolomei had given it, Vetta d'Italia (Summit of Italy), it is the northernmost point of the Italian Republic's territory. The grandiose panorama from the pinnacle encompasses the Grossglockner, the highest mountain in Austria, to the east and an array of other Alpine giants.

༄

THE FATE OF PRINCESSES

The village of Dietenheim/Teodorone on a local road less than 1 mile (1.3 kilometers) northeast of Bruneck/Brunico houses the South Tyrolean Museum of Local Ethnic Traditions, 24 Herzog-Diet-Strasse, on 6.5 acres (3 hectares) of land. The main building is a three-hundred-year-old gabled former dairy farm, Mair am Hof, with a barn and stables across its courtyard. Around this nucleus several buildings—transferred from various other locations in the region where for different reasons they could no longer remain—have been reassembled over the past eighteen years. Thus the old dairy complex now faces other ancient farmhouses, the dwellings of small-property owners, a sawmill and a flour mill, a smithy, and mountain refuge huts. Authentic period furniture and implements are on display in the wood-beamed and paneled rooms. The museum can be visited 9:30 A.M.–5:30 P.M. Tuesday to Saturday, 2–6 P.M. Sunday, from mid-April to the end of October.

Proceeding eastward on National Route 49, after the charming summer resort of Welsberg/Monguelfo, one reaches a wooded district and the mouth of the Prags/Braies Valley, which runs southward.

High up in this side valley, 7.5 miles (12 kilometers) southwest of the turnoff from Route 49, is what many regard as the most beautiful lake in the entire Alps. It is known as the Pragser Wildsee/Lago di Braies. At an altitude of 4,898 feet (1,493 meters), tall spruce trees surround the aquamarine, clear, and cold body of water, which mirrors the jagged rock walls of the Seeko-fel/Croda del Becco, which rises to the south of it at a height of 9,219 feet (2,810 meters).

The lake is .75 mile (1.2 kilometers) long and up to .25 mile (400 meters) wide. Boats may be rented. A forty-five- to sixty-minute walk on a lovely tree-lined path around the lake affords ever-new vistas from the clearings. On the western shore, near the long-established Braies/Pragser Wildsee Hotel, stands a little church. The lake, formed in prehistoric times by a rock slide from the 7,933-foot (2,418-meter) Herrnstein/Rocca del Signore mountain, is quite deep—117 feet (35.7 meters) at one point. Divers who went to the bottom and took pictures found that the lake floor didn't look as pretty as the surface; it was littered with debris, such as a discarded boiler and a toilet bowl. Efforts are under way, promoted by the region's Green movement, to clean up not only the lake of Prags/Braies, but all Alpine lakes. The best times to visit the Pragser Wildsee/Lago di Braies are outside the peak tourist seasons.

Whoever leaves the Prags/Braies Valley, or has passed it up to continue an eastward trip on Route 49, might stop briefly at Niederdorf/Villabassa, a resort village on a forested shelf with some old patrician mansions. One of them is the arcaded Wasser-mann House. A period inscription on the landmarked building records that Isabella of Parma, a granddaughter of King Louis XV of France, rested here on her way to Vienna in 1760. She was to become the wife of Crown Prince Joseph of Hapsburg, who would soon be coemperor with his mother, Maria Theresa.

The beautiful, accomplished, and intellectual princess, who also bore the title Infanta of Spain, is one of the most intriguing figures of the Rococo era. Barely nineteen years old at the time of her solemn wedding in Vienna, she charmed the Hapsburg court by her tact even more than with her pretty singing voice and her skills in painting and playing the clavichord and violin. The crown prince adored his young wife; she bore him two daughters, but they died soon. Isabella herself succumbed to small-pox in 1763; Joseph II never forgot her.

Today we know from Isabella's posthumous papers that she was an early feminist, was unhappy in her marriage, and found solace in Vienna in a passionate love affair with a sister of her husband, Archduchess Maria Christina. Isabella's written legacy, all in French, includes a treatise, *On Men*, that seems to anticipate the themes of the women's liberation movement, and an essay, *On the Fate of Princesses*, in which she deplored the fact that the daughter of a sovereign was from her birth surrounded by cabals and would eventually be traded off in some political marriage. From a great number of intimate letters to her sister-in-law that have been conserved, it would appear that what was going on between Isabella and Maria Christina was more than just a roman-tic, exalted friendship.

I had long been fascinated by the French-Spanish-Italian princess but hadn't known about her stay in the Pustertal until I saw the old inscription. The Niederdorfers must have been quite taken with the beautiful young woman who, they thought, would become their empress. Recently the village bought the

Wassermann House and intends to create a South Tyrolean Tourist Museum in it.

From Niederdorf it is only 2.5 miles (4 kilometers) to the highest point of both Route 49 and the Pustertal/Val Pusteria railroad line. It is the watershed between the Rienza and Drava Rivers.

The flat, wide saddle at an altitude of 3,983 feet (1,214 meters) is a crossroads: to the right (south) is an important gateway to the Dolomites, National Route 51; a road to the left, across the fields, leads to Old Toblach on a gentle incline. Neu Toblach/ Dobbiaco Nuovo, south of the rail station, consists mainly of hotels, pensions, and eating places. The narrow-gauge Dolomite railway that used to run from Toblach/Dobbiaco to Cortina d'Ampezzo and on to Calalzo di Cadore in Belluno Province has long ended operations, to be superseded by bus service.

Sights in Old Toblach include the parish church in Baroque-Rococo style, with a tall, isolated steeple, and an old aristocratic mansion nearby called the Herbstenburg after Herbst, a chamberlain of Emperor Maximilian I, who purchased it in 1500 and had it altered to his tastes. Toblach/Dobbiaco also has a Gustav Mahler Street, a Mahler Monument in the main square, and a summer festival named after the composer, the Mahler Music Weeks.

જૂ

MAHLER'S COMPOSING SHACK

Gustav Mahler spent the last summers before his death in a farming manor of the Dolomite Road between Toblach and the hamlet of Schluderbach/Carbonin. He moved to the place near Toblach in late summer 1907 after his older daughter, Maria Anna, died of scarlet fever and diphtheria at Maiernigg on the Woerth Lake in Carinthia. He had been inhabiting a summer house there for five years but did not want to live in it any longer after the deeply traumatic loss of his and his wife Alma's first child at the age of four.

The year of 1907 was an ominous one for Mahler. In Vienna, where he had been court opera director for nearly ten years, the intrigues of artistic and bureaucratic jealousy being spun around him turned nastier than usual. After his daughter's funeral he suffered what may have been a heart attack, and doctors diagnosed a serious cardiac ailment. Eventually he reluctantly resigned his prestigious court opera post, accepting an offer from the Metropolitan Opera in New York. In December 1907 he left for America.

Mahler was back in the new summer place near Toblach in 1908 for one of his working vacations. For several years the long operatic seasons in Vienna and his concert engagements had left Mahler only July and August for composing; he would complete the instrumentation of his scores in Vienna whenever he found time. The vacation home of the composer, his wife, and their younger daughter, Anna Justine, south of Toblach was a vast apartment with a closed veranda on the second floor of a fifteenth-century residence, the Trenker Hof. Dolomite walls and peaks are all around the spot.

For his composing Mahler needed absolute quiet, which he found in a little wooden shack with a gabled roof in a forest of tall spruce trees a five-minute walk from the Trenker Hof. Nobody was allowed to come near it when he was at work, often in shirtsleeves, from time to time trying out a musical phrase on the piano. The Viennese painter Carl Moll, Alma Mahler's stepfather, sketched the "composing cabin" during a visit.

With the evergreen trees around him and glimpses of the Dolomite mountains through them, Mahler composed *Das Lied von der Erde* (*The Song of the Earth*) in summer 1908. It is a cycle for two singing voices using German renderings of ancient Chinese poetry by Li Po, Wang Wei, and others.

In the summer of 1909 Mahler completed his Ninth Symphony in the "composing cabin," and in 1910 he wrote there the opening adagio of his unfinished Tenth Symphony. The scherzo in the Ninth is based on a *Ländler*, the uncontrived folk dance of Austrian farm people from which the waltz developed. The fragment of the Tenth is full of emotional melodic skips. According to his wife, the composer drew her attention to a leaping passage and explained that "the Dolomites are dancing this with one another." Yet the overall impression of Mahler's Dolomite compositions is a mood of existential crisis with forebodings of death, accepted with resignation.

Maybe Mahler, in his gloomier moments, would not have been all too surprised if he had been told that the very spot where he was writing his music would in a few years witness the horrors of war. Most of Schluderbach was indeed flattened in fighting between Austrians and Italians, 1915–18. World War I artillery positions and infantry trenches can still be seen today within walking distance from the long rebuilt hamlet. The Trenker Hof is today an inn and cafe with a few rooms for skiers and hikers, as well as a Mahler Memorial Room, the composer's former living room, with a piano.

While Mahler was working in his composing hut, his flirtatious wife, as she told much later in her memoirs, engaged in a dalliance with a houseguest, the young pianist Ossip Gabrilowitsch; yet the virtuoso, gentleman through and through, left after their first kiss. A few years after Mahler's death in Vienna in 1911 Alma was back in the Dolomites, this time with the painter Oskar Kokoschka at the height of their tempestuous love affair. It is not clear whether the pair visited the hamlet where Alma had spent parts of four summers with Mahler and their daughter; Schluderbach is just 12 miles (19 kilometers) from the Dolomite capital, Cortina d'Ampezzo.

♋

MOUNTAINEERING
AND SKI PARADISE

From Toblach/Dobbiaco it takes only 2.5 miles (4 kilometers) on Route 49 to Innichen/San Candido, a 1,200-year-old market town scenically located at the entrance to the Sexten/Sesto side valley. Scores of hotels, inns, pensions, and restaurants in and around Innichen and the nearby village of Sexten show that this is a much frequented tourist and winter sports district.

Innichen/San Candido boasts a major architectural and artistic sight, the Abbey Church of St. Candidus and St. Corbinian. The Romanesque edifice in the cemetery behind the parish church was built in the thirteenth century at the site of an early-medieval Benedictine monastery, which around the year 1200 was destroyed by fire. The south portal, called the Venetian Gate, opens under an outdoor fresco attributed to Michael Pacher (circa 1480), representing the church's patron saints with Emperor Otto the Great (912–973) between them. The emperor had favored the old abbey.

Walk around the outside of the choir to have a good look at the muscular architecture of the remarkable building. Inside, the veneration of the faithful centers on the Innichen cross above the main altar—a seven-hundred-year-old wooden sculpture representing a hieratic and crowned crucified Christ, his feet resting on Adam's head, flanked by Mary and John. Frescoes in the square dome, which came to light during restoration work in the 1960s, date from the thirteenth century, picturing scenes from the biblical Creation story. Near the church stands one of the oldest houses in the entire Pustertal/Val Pusteria, a stone building with battlements and Gothic windows, containing a library of theological works, the archives of the church's former chapter, and a museum illustrating the history of the old abbey and church. The museum can be visited 10 a.m.–noon and 5–7 P.M. Saturday and Sunday between the beginning of June and the end of October.

Innichen/San Candido is an excellent base for excursions into the mountaineering, trekking, and ski paradise of the Sexten/Sesto Valley and into Austria's East Tyrol.

The Drava River rises inconspicuously in the mountains southwest of the town and is soon reinforced by the Sextenbach (Sexten Brook) rushing down from the Dolomites. National Route 52, starting at Innichen/San Candido, runs along that stream to climb the Dolomite passes and proceed into the Cadore mountains. The highway first traverses a forest and 4 miles (about 7 kilometers) from Innichen reaches the village of Sexten/Sesto in a beautiful spot where the valley widens, surrounded by dark pine forests and surmounted by the steep 7,982-foot (2,433-meter) Mount Helm to the east and even mightier Dolomite peaks to the west. Sexten was almost completely destroyed during World War I and was rebuilt afterward. The mountain farmers returned to their precariously located properties when the fighting was over. The war experiences inspired a *Dance of Death* fresco that the Bolzano-born artist Rudolf Stolz (1874–1960) painted on a circular structure at the village cemetery.

The hamlet of Moos/Moso, a little more than 1 mile (2 kilometers) from Sexten, is particularly lovely, snuggling in a little green hollow where the Fischlein/Fiscalina torrent joins the Sexten Brook. Nearly every one of the broad wooden houses is either an inn or is inhabited by a peasant family that takes in paying guests. The panorama of the high mountains all around is stunning; there is an abundance of ski lifts around Sexten and Moos. From Route 52 a branch road on the right (west) side leads up to Bad Moos/Bagni di Moso, a mountain spa at 4,485 feet (1,367 meters) above sea level with a sulphur spring and a group of hotels.

From the upper Fischlein/Fiscalina Valley experienced rock climbers set out to scale one of the "three pinnacles," the Drei Zinnen/Tre Cime di Lavaredo. These are a daunting trio of Dolomite blocks soaring to 9,370, 9,754, and 9,836 feet (2,856, 2,973 and 2,998 meters) altitude. Mountain refuges are at their approaches.

The Italian-Austrian frontier is 5 miles (8 kilometers) east of Innichen/San Candido at the village of Winnebach/Prato alla Drava. Beyond this Italian outpost lies East Tyrol, which administratively belongs to the Austrian region of Tyrol. The Italian National Route 49 becomes Austrian Route B 100; the bilingual signs end, but the traveler is still in the Pustertal, the railroad tracks and the highway following the upper Drava River, which in Austria is called the Drau.

Coming from Italy, with Mount Helm to one's right, one soon reaches the market town of Sillian, at 3,537 feet (1,078 meters) above sea level. The valley seems less densely populated than it is on the Italian side; it narrows after about 20 miles (32 kilometers) from the border, forming a gorge, the Lienzer Klause, that marks the end of the Pustertal. Beyond the gorge the young Drava receives plenty of water from the glaciers and snow fields on the Alpine main crest that the Isel torrent furnishes; the further course of the merged rivers is known as the Ober-Drautal (Upper Drava Valley).

ॐ

LOFTY ROAD

The two rivers, Drava and Isel, join in a broad basin, enclosing the city of Lienz, the capital of East Tyrol. With a population of twelve thousand, it makes a modern impression although the Town Hall on the main square, Hauptplatz, north of the railroad station is from the sixteenth century, and there are a few old churches. Toward the south, the city looks out on the Lienz Dolomites, with rugged peaks of up to 9,000 feet (more than 2,700 meters) altitude.

A landmark is Bruck Castle on the slope of a forested hill northwest of Lienz, which can be reached in a fifteen-minute stroll. The stronghold, with a mighty keep, once controlled the mouth of the Isel Valley; it was built in the thirteenth century on what is believed to have been the site of an ancient Roman fortress. During the Middle Ages the castle was one of the residences of the powerful counts of Görz, a noble family with possessions in a wide Alpine area; its name is perpetuated in the Italian city and provincial capital of Gorizia (German: Görz) between Udine and Trieste, where the counts also had a large castle.

Proceeding eastward from Lienz, the traveler soon passes an excavation site with traces of the once flourishing Roman merchant town of Aguntum. It was founded in the first century A.D., played an important and lucrative role in the trade between the Roman Empire's Alpine provinces and the rich south for more than four hundred years, and was looted and destroyed by barbarian invaders sometime in the sixth century. A dozen generations of Roman officials and Latinized provincial businesspeople lived and died in Aguntum, and we know hardly anything about them.

A little farther to the east, about 4 miles (7 kilometers) from Lienz, is the turnoff to Route B 107, the Grossglockner Road. During the warm months B 107 represents a spectacular connection between East Tyrol and the Salzburg region just below some of the highest peaks in the Alps.

Ascending a northern side valley of the Drava, the highway reaches the picture-postcard village of Heiligenblut in little more than 20 miles (37 kilometers). Situated in a green cove, it is a cluster of houses around a fifteenth-century church with a slender, tapering steeple. The shrine's tabernacle holds a revered vial said to treasure a drop of the Holy Blood of Jesus (whence the village's name). The relic is believed to have been brought from Constantinople in the tenth century by a saintly man, identified as the Blessed Briccius. The church's high altar is noteworthy for a colored-and-gilt group representing the Coronation of the Virgin, executed in 1520 by a wood-carver from the school of Michael Pacher of Bruneck.

Heiligenblut was once a mining town; gold and silver were brought to light in the mountains overlooking it, the Hohe Tauern. Today the village, which belongs to the Austrian region of Carinthia, has found a new mine in tourism, especially since the opening of the Hochalpenstrasse (High Alpine Road) across the Hohe Tauern in 1935. The best view of the white pyramid of the Grossglockner, Austria's tallest mountain with an altitude of 12,457 feet (3,797 meters), is obtained from Schuler Hill, a raised point a few minutes' stroll southeast of the village.

The Grossglockner toll road is open from May to October or November, depending on the weather. It rises in many narrow curves to an altitude of 8,218 feet (2,505 meters) with an inclination of 12 percent in some sections and is not recommended for vehicles with trailers. Cars with stick shifts are by far preferable to ones with automatic gearshifts. Panoramic platforms command magnificent vistas of the mountain peaks and the largest glacier in the eastern Alps, a nearly 6-mile (9-kilometer) ice stream known as the Pasterze.

Soon past Heiligenblut a branch road mounts for 5 miles (8 kilometers) westward to the Franz Joseph Height, 7,772 feet (2,369 meters) above sea level, a spot from which Emperor Franz Joseph admired the glacier panorama and the Grossglockner summit in 1856. Refreshments, meals, and accommodations are offered by the Alpenhotel Franz-Josef-Haus.

The Grossglockner Road passes its highest point in a tunnel, the Hochtor (High Gate). A little beyond it, another side ramp leads up eastward to a second panoramic lookout, the Edelweiss Spitze (Edelweiss Point), at an altitude of 8,451 feet (2,576 meters). A little more than 20 miles (33 kilometers) from Heiligenblut, after another series of switchbacks, the Grossglockner Road joins Route B 168 in the valley of the Salzach River at the village of Bruck; proceed eastward to Salzburg or westward to Innsbruck.

Practiced Alpinists who disdain motorized mountain tourism climb the Grossglockner with or without a guide in eight hours or more from Heiligenblut or from the village of Kals, which is reached over Route B 108 from Lienz. Various mountain refuges provide food and shelter.

✍

SUNNY LAKE COUNTRY

Travelers who aren't tempted by the Grossglockner Road and pass the turnoff to Heiligenblut to go straight on Route B 100 down the Drava Valley enter Carinthia some 12 miles (20 kilometers) east of Lienz. Carinthia is the southernmost and sunniest of Austria's nine self-governing regions; the area has a sizable Slovenian minority, and in some Carinthian villages Slovenian is heard spoken and often sung. Slovenians are renowned for their choirs.

Route B 100 connects with a spur of Motorway A-10 from Salzburg to Villach at the village of Möllbrücke, 43 miles (69 kilometers) east of Lienz. From there it is another 21 miles (33 kilometers) on Route B 100 or on Motorway A-10 in a wide, green valley to the city of Villach near the Italian border.

With about fifty thousand inhabitants, Villach is Carinthia's dynamic second city after Klagenfurt, a center of the timber trade and other exchanges with neighboring Slovenia and Italy. The Old Town on the south bank of the Drava River has its heart in the elongated Hauptplatz (Main Square) with a Trinity Column and, at its southern end, the parish Church of St. Jacob, from the fifteenth century, with a detached, high tower. Much of the city was destroyed in heavy Allied air raids aimed at the railroad yards during World War II and has been rebuilt since then.

A spa complex, Warmbad Villach, is 2.5 miles (4 kilometers)

158

south of the city center and has its own railroad station. Its outdoor and indoor swimming pools and its elaborate facilities for hydrotherapy are fed by hot springs (86 degrees Fahrenheit or 30 centigrade). Villach looks out on the dark rocks of the Karawanken chain, which separates Carinthia from Slovenia. The frontiers of Austria, Italy, and Slovenia converge at a marker west of the 3,520-foot (1,073-meter) Wurzen Pass, a steep gateway to Upper Slovenia under which most traffic moves through a 4.5-mile (7-kilometer) tunnel today.

The railroad line, highway, and motorway turn from Villach southwest and cross the Austrian-Italian border between the double village of Thörl-Maglern and the town of Tarvisio, a winter sports center and summer resort. From Tarvisio the rail line, Motorway A-23 (Italian), and National Route 13 continue to Udine, the capital of the Friuli region, in 56 miles (90 kilometers) and in another 78 miles (125 kilometers) to Venice.

Taking Motorway A-2 (Austrian) or National Route B 83 eastward, you will soon be driving along the scenic north shore of Lake Woerth (Woerther See), which is more than 10 miles (17 kilometers) long and up to almost 1 mile (1.5 kilometers) wide. Fine views of the lake are also obtained from the railroad between Villach and Klagenfurt. For motorists, an alternative is the highway along the lake's southern shore, from the elegant resort town of Velden to the village of Maria Woerth on a short peninsula and on to Klagenfurt.

The lake freezes over partially or entirely during harsh winters but receives copious sunshine in summer. The resorts on its north side, with impressive views of the Karawanken range across the water and of Maria Woerth, form together a Carinthian Riviera with many hotels, pensions, restaurants, cafes, and discotheques. Velden has a gambling casino and is close to a golf course.

As a student I once swam across the lake from the resort village of Krumpendorf but wasn't too sure I would make it to the south shore and faint-heartedly had asked local friends to accompany me in a rowboat. When I was at the other side they congratulated me on my feat with straight faces, and I proudly returned to Krumpendorf in their boat. Only later did I learn that my escorts used to swim across the lake and back again by day and night without any boat, and I realized they had been making fun of me.

Klagenfurt, a city of ninety thousand, spreads in a vast basin near the eastern end of Lake Woerth. The seat of the regional government, it is a quiet center of bureaucrats and mostly well-to-do professional and businesspeople. Its main sight is the sixteenth-century Dragon Fountain on Neuer Platz (New Square), representing a legendary monster that was said to have had its lair in the then swampy plain in times of old. The eighteenth-century City Hall is on the west side of the lengthy central square.

From Klagenfurt it is about four hours by train or car to Vienna, which is some 200 miles (320 kilometers) north of the Carinthian capital via the A-2. Klagenfurt Airport is less than 2 miles (1.5 kilometers) from the city center.

Even more picturesque than Lake Woerth, and in summer equally popular with holidaymakers, are Carinthia's several smaller lakes, especially the Lake of Ossiach and the Lake of Millstatt, both easily reachable on good highways from the lower Drava Valley and Villach.

VII.

EASYGOING
LADINIA

∽

A narrow and unsightly concrete bridge 14 miles (23 kilometers) north of Bolzano doesn't seem to make any effort to
lure travelers to the village of Ponte Gardena/Waidbruck on the
east bank of the Eisack/Isarco River, yet it is the main entrance
to splendid Ladinia. The name *Ladinia* is unofficial, denoting
the valleys, villages, and green hillsides, surmounted by rugged
Dolomite bastions and peaks, where Ladin is spoken.

Ladinia starts close to Ponte Gardena/Waidbruck, but not
quite there. Beyond that concrete bridge—which is soon to be
made obsolete by another, broader river crossing a little downstream—the visitor has a choice among three roads. The middle
one, National Route 242, leads into Gherdëina, which is the
Ladin name for what Tyroleans call the Grödental and the Italians
Val Gardena; it is the principal Ladin valley.

To the right is a provincial road rising to the town of Kastel-
ruth/Castelrotto and the Schlern/Sciliar massif, which will be
described on page 175. A footpath, close to the highway, climbs
from the small village of Waidbruck to a well-preserved medieval
stronghold on a rock spur some 350 feet (130 meters) higher up.
It is the Trostburg, which once controlled the Brenner Road
and access to the Ladin valleys. Trostburg may come from the

Ladin word *troi*, meaning "path" or "road." The castle belonged for centuries to the aristocratic Wolkenstein family, and it may or may not have been the birthplace of the minnesinger Oswald von Wolkenstein (1367–1445), the one-eyed adventurer, poet, and far-traveled diplomat, whom we shall encounter later in this chapter (page 178).

The Trostburg, which Italians call Castello Forte (Strong Castle), is a redoubtable fortress that would be the perfect setting for a gothic novel or a costume film. Some of its walls are 6.5 feet (2 meters) thick, its square keep and its other towers are massive, and it is well protected by moats and outworks. A Gothic Hall from the fifteenth century, and the long and narrow seventeenth-century Hall of Knights with a beamed ceiling in carved wood, stuccoed walls, and statues of Wolkenstein counts, are above a maze of chambers, halls, corridors, stairways, and basement vaults on various levels. The Trostburg can be visited in guided tours morning and afternoon, Tuesday to Saturday, from Easter to the end of October.

Another provincial road goes up in scenic curves from the north side of Ponte Gardena/Waidbruck to the very old village of Lajen/Laion at 3,586 feet (1,093 meters) above sea level with magnificent views of the Gherdëina Dolomites to the east. In past centuries Lajen was the seat of a law court and a parish, both with jurisdiction over other Ladin villages; now few of the inhabitants understand Ladin. Today the sloping village with two ancient churches and several old houses is a quiet summer resort. Below Lajen, in a location called Ried, stands the old farmhouse that is the presumed birthplace of Walther von der Vogelweide (page 61).

The provincial road between Ponte Gardena/Waidbruck and Lajen crosses Route 242 dir. (the abbreviation stands for *diramazi-*

one, or branch), which provides an alternative access to Ladinia from a point on the Brenner highway north of Klausen/Chiusa and joins the principal Route 242 at the hamlet of Pontives near Urtijëi/Ortisei/St.Ulrich. This arm of the highway essentially follows the former roadbed of a narrow-gauge railroad line that linked Klausen with the upper Gherdëina Valley.

Austria-Hungary built the Gherdëina railroad after Italy's entry into World War I in 1915 to transport troops, ammunition, and other military supplies to its new Dolomite front. The line started at Klausen station and in 19 miles (31 kilometers), with many curves, viaducts, and seven tunnels, rose from 1,765 feet (538 meters) to the hamlet of Plan at an altitude of 5,269 feet (1,606 meters). From Plan, improvised cableways took the soldiers and shipments to the lofty battlefield on the Dolomite heights. In six months' feverish work, 3,500 soldiers and 6,000 Russian prisoners of war under the direction of 500 engineers completed the major part of the railroad, which started functioning in 1916 and was finished in 1917. After World War I it continued as a civilian passenger and freight operation.

The Gherdëina railroad was much beloved by local people and even inspired poetry and songs. I took it a few times in the 1950s, making sure to sit on the right side of the little wooden coach, which offered the best views. In some stretches the twigs and foliage of trees would reach inside through the open windows. In 1960 the Italian state railways discontinued the line, which had long been unprofitable. The tracks were torn out, but miles of the old roadbed remain recognizable and serve at present as promenades and as biking and jogging tracks. Public buses today connect all towns and major villages of Ladinia with Bolzano and other regional centers.

A salvaged steam locomotive with a red front shield and red

undercarriage that once plied the line sits on a length of narrow-gauge track near a children's playground at the end of the Luis Trenker Promenade east of the parish church of Urtijëi. The engine, No. 410004, was discovered in the early 1970s on a dead-end track of a marshaling yard in Rome, ready for sale as scrap iron. The town of Urtijëi bought it in 1973 and put it up as a memorial of the unforgotten little railroad.

Far above the former roadbed of the Gherdëina railroad and the present Route 242 dir., along the mountain ranges and across the forests, snakes a primeval footpath, called in Ladin Troi Paian (Heathens' Path). In prehistoric times it provided communication between remote Dolomite valleys and a rudimentary Brenner Road. In 1830 a bronze dagger, tentatively dated sometime between 1300 and 800 B.C., was found below the ancient path.

The original route 242 from Ponte Gardena/Waidbruck is the most impressive way of penetrating Ladinia. It runs along the Gherdëina stream (Grödenbach in German), which near the concrete bridge joins the Eisack/Isarco. Right after Ponte Gardena the road traverses a ravine, then mounts in bends toward the hamlet of Pontives, where it merges with Route 242 dir. Another rocky defile after Pontives is called the Ladin Gate: beyond it Ladin is spoken.

∽

MILLENNIUM CELEBRATION

Emerging from the gorge, one beholds a beautiful large basin surrounded by green slopes; far to the east rises the jagged gray rock pillar of the Saslonch (Long Stone)/Langkofel and the nearly square, immense Dolomite block of the Sella massif. The town spreading in the middle of the bowl through which the Gherdëina stream flows has three official names: Urtijëi, Ortisei, and St. Ulrich. At 4,055 feet (1,236 meters) above sea level, with 4,500 permanent inhabitants, it is the main center of the Gherdëina Valley and the capital of Ladinia.

The German name of the town is that of the patron saint of its parish church, St. Ulrich (Ladin: St. Huldrych), bishop of Augsburg (890–973), who successfully defended the Bavarian city against Hungarian raiders. In the Middle Ages the wealthy bishopric of Augsburg had possessions in the Gherdëina Valley and sometime around the year 1000 erected a chapel there, dedicating it to St. Ulrich. The town's coat of arms shows the figure of the sainted bishop sitting on a rearing white steed, holding a cross in his right hand.

On July 4, 1993, I happened to be revisiting Urtijëi, unaware that Independence Day in the United States, falling that year on a Sunday, was also the feast day of St. Ulrich in the Ladin town. Firecrackers going off on the mountainsides all around in the early morning and the pealing of all church bells later announced a major celebration. A Ladin friend told me with a chuckle: "We are a thousand years old."

The clergy and the town fathers had in fact decided to proclaim "One Thousand Years Urtijëi" on the assumption, not supported by any written source, that the bishopric of Augsburg created its ecclesiastic outpost in the Gherdëina Valley in A.D. 993. It was an auspicious start to another great summer tourist season.

Red-white Tyrolean and yellow-white Vatican flags fluttered from many houses in the town. I didn't see any Italian green-white-red tricolors. From below the onion dome of the parish church's steeple and from the edifice's gable hung only Vatican banners.

The parish church, in late-Baroque style, was built in 1797 and enlarged later. The interior is overdecorated with mediocre paintings and with many statues and sculptures by local wood-carvers.

High mass was sung in the crowded church with six priests concelebrating and swarms of altar boys in attendance. Prayers, responses, and chants were in Latin, German, and Ladin. After the hour-long service a procession emerged from the church's little porch amid the booms of another salvo of powerful fire-crackers set off on a nearby slope.

First came the Urtijëi voluntary firemen in their brown uniforms with glittering helmets, carrying their gold-embroidered banner with them. They were followed by a troop of children in Gherdëina costumes. The boys were in leather breeches with white stockings and buckled shoes; they wore green jackets over red waistcoats and sported broad-brimmed green hats. The girls walked in long, dark skirts with white blouses and kerchiefs; they had broad black velvet ribbons across their foreheads and wore little crowns of gilt metal and colored glass. Among them was a tiny African beauty, also in Ladin dress—the adopted daughter of a local family.

Swedish tourists whose bus had been held up by the procession couldn't seem to get enough camera shots of the Gherdëina belles. Carabinieri in their tan summer uniforms and municipal policemen in white tunics and black trousers held up traffic and cleared the way for the marchers.

The costumed children were followed by delegations from other Ladin villages and hamlets, also in their traditional dress.

Most of the women wore wide-brimmed green hats over black velvet headbands, white embroidered kerchiefs, and green bodices trimmed with gaudy ribbons over long-sleeved white blouses; their blue, green, or violet long skirts were also adorned with bright ribbons. Some older women sported high pyramid-shaped dark blue wool caps with a brighter blue bow on top. The men wore broad green hats, green jackets, leather breeches, white stockings, and buckled shoes. Their belts were broad, and some had old silver coins dangling from them.

A group of Urtijëi notables came afterward. The men wore decorous green frock coats and black high hats, the women long skirts, golden belts, laced-up bodices, and broad green or black hats.

The burghers' section was followed by the town band, also in Gherdëina dress, playing hymns that sounded like dirges. An athletic young fellow walking behind the music carried a church banner, large like a sheet for a king-size bed and slit into stripes so that the wind wouldn't catch it like a sail; other young men held ropes to keep the banner from toppling or being blown away by a sudden gust. Behind them eight sturdy youths carried the giant gilt-wood statue of St. Ulrich that normally stands in the church. It represents the enthroned patron saint as a bearded man wearing a bishop's miter, his right arm raised in the gesture of blessing.

Altar boys in red-and-white garb preceded the clergy. The parish priest of Urtijëi, in a gold-embroidered cope, had his aged predecessor at his side, a Slovenian who during his many years of ministry in the Ladin town had won great popularity and had retired a few years earlier, continuing to help out in the church. Hundreds of civilians in their Sunday best, shuffling behind the praying and chanting ecclesiastics, brought up the rear.

Meanwhile, many Italian, German, and other summer guests had joined the Swedes on the sidelines, working their cameras. The foreigners seemed to think they were being treated to one of the folklore shows that summer resorts stage for the benefit of tourists. Urtijëi too offers such shows every season. This time, however, the mood was different—the townspeople were celebrating for themselves. I was struck by an unusual solemnity; the faces of the marchers were serious: they appeared to be conscious and proud of a millenary tradition.

The procession toured the town center and passed the little seventeenth-century Church of St. Anthony (which the local Roman Catholic clergy lends to the Protestants for Sunday services). At the main square near the Cësa di Ladins (House of Ladins), the marchers turned around and up the sloping Streda Rezia (Rhaetian Street) and went back to the parish church, where they disbanded. Soon the town's taverns started filling up.

MOTHER'S LANGUAGE

The Cësa di Ladins, opened in 1960, is the cultural center of Ladinia. On the wall to the left of its main entrance four lines in Gothic (black-letter) script read:

> *Gherdëina, Gherdëina*
> *De L'oma si rujné*
> *Rejona, rejona*
> *Y no te l dejmincé!*
> *(Gherdëina, Gherdëina*

Your mother's language
Speak, speak
And don't forget it!)

The verses are a stanza of a poem by the Ladin writer Leo Runggaldier-Furdenán (1888–1961), whose grave is in the Urtijëi cemetery. His exhortation to save the ancient tongue from oblivion has become the official anthem of the Gherdëina Ladins.

Some thirty thousand inhabitants of five valleys and nearby areas today speak Ladin, at least in their homes. Italians have long tended to regard Ladin as merely a hillbilly dialect of their own tongue, but local scholars contend that the Ladin branch of the Rhaeto-Romance group of languages is by no means a descendant of Italian, but essentially a direct derivation from Latin.

The Ladins were for centuries loyal subjects of the Austrian emperors and during World War I fought against the Italians side by side with other Austrio-Hungarian soldiers on the Dolomite front. After World War I, Ladin leaders petitioned in vain the Allied statesmen attending the Paris peace conference to allow their people to remain with the Austrian Tyrol. During the first few years after the war, the Ladins affirmed in public manifestations to be a self-contained ethnic community and displayed a banner of their own—blue, white, and green with an edelweiss flower at its center.

The Fascist regime would not admit that there was a separate Ladin identity. Yet when Hitler and Mussolini agreed in 1939 that German-speaking residents of Bolzano Province and adjacent districts could choose to emigrate to greater Germany, the Ladins found themselves included among those declared eligible. This was tantamount to an acknowledgment that they weren't really Italians, although Ladins who decided to stay on, like German speakers who did, would have to consider themselves Italian citizens in every respect. Few Ladins opted for German citizenship and emigration, and World War II put an end to the people transfer.

After the downfall of Mussolini and restoration of democracy in Italy, the majority of Ladins supported the South Tyrolean People's Party and regional autonomy in all elections. In 1972 the Ladins of Bolzano Province won legal recognition as a separate ethnic group. A *lista di ladins*, or Ladin ticket, was presented in various local elections, although the majority of the Ladin community kept voting for the South Tyrolean People's Party.

The Ladin language is now taught in the schools of the Ladin valleys and heard on local radio and television programs. Ladins have their own representatives in the regional bodies.

For the foreign visitor it's not easy to identify Ladins immediately. They aren't a pugnacious minority and blend unobtrusively with their environment. Virtually all of them also speak the Tyrolean dialect of German, and many have a good to perfect mastery of Italian as well. The Tyroleans have long referred to their Ladin fellow residents as *Krautwalsche*, an ethnic label meaning something like Italians who eat sauerkraut as they do themselves. To the uninitiated, Ladin traditional folk costumes worn on festive occasions look like the Tyrolean ones; only experts will note the small, telling particularities, like the little crownlike hats of the girls.

Through the centuries the unassertive Ladin farmers and artisans have managed to get along with everybody. They have a reputation for hard work and reliability, are polite with strangers, like order and cleanliness, and are fond of socializing and laughter. They are renowned wood-carvers and often excel in other visual arts and in music. Good voices can be heard from the choir lofts of their churches during Sunday services. All this contributes to Ladinia's special, relaxed atmosphere.

The Cësa di Ladins of Urtijëi houses the office of a cultural organization, a library, and the Museum of Gherdëina. An archaeological collection contains the bronze dagger that was found below the Heathens' Path. The weapon's handle, one piece with the stabbing part, is ornamented with geometrical patterns. There are also other prehistoric artifacts.

One room is filled with mineral samples, old photos, a butterfly collection, and stuffed animals, including an albino deer; the rare white animal was shot in 1960 by a hunter in a hillside forest close to Urtijëi.

The main part of the museum is devoted to products of local handicrafts and to works by old and modern Gherdëina artists— wood carvings, sculptures, toys, and paintings. The Gherdëina Museum, 83 Streda Rezia, is open 10 A.M.–noon and 3–7 P.M. daily in July and August, 3–6:30 P.M. Tuesday to Friday in June and from September 1 to October 8.

⁂

WOOD-CARVERS

An idea of what local wood-carvers at present have to offer may be obtained from the Permanent Exhibition of Gherdëina Artistic Handicrafts on the ground floor of the modern Congress Building on Church Square, corner Streda Rezia. It is open 10 A.M.–noon and 3–7 P.M. Monday to Saturday in July and August, 3–6 P.M. in June. Admission is free.

Wood carving is an age-old art, practiced all over the world, especially in areas where timber is plentiful. In the Alps with their abundant forests, settlers have since the earliest times whiled away the long winter evenings fashioning wood blocks into household articles, toys, and sculptures. Tyrolean artistic wood carving brought forth such Renaissance masters as the Pachers of Bruneck.

As a cottage industry, wood carving in the Gherdëina Valley goes back to the early eighteenth century. Many of the estimated 3,500 people who then lived in Urtijëi, the nearby hamlets, and the many isolated farmsteads on the slopes would whittle at pinewood at home when they hadn't to look after their cattle or fields. They produced statues of biblical figures and saints, figurines for crèches, toy animals, picture frames, and many other things.

The Ladin valley was then to a degree cut off from the outside world, but its industrious and frugal inhabitants nevertheless managed to market their artifacts abroad. As early as two hundred years ago a few enterprising villagers acted as agents, buying up wood carvings from the family workshops and taking them in backpacks over footpaths and mule tracks to dealers in towns beyond the mountain ridges. The commerce became so lucrative that even children seven or eight years old helped their elders in carving and coloring their wooden sculptures. Small wonder that wielding the wood knife and scraper seem inborn skills of the Gherdëina Ladins.

Wood carving became a veritable valley industry after the highway from Waidbruck/Ponte Gardena to Urtijëi, today the initial section of Route 242, was opened in 1856. Gherdëina wood sculptures were sold all over central Europe and northern Italy. By 1890 two dozen professional wood-carving workshops with up to twenty full-time workers each flourished in Urtijëi.

The traveler is at present greeted by wood-sculpture businesses lining the highway a mile before the first houses of Urtijëi. Some deal only with wholesalers. Scores of shops on the town's main street and on side lanes offer wood carvings, and the hiker who climbs the nearby mountain paths will every now and then come to a sign "BILDHAUER—SCULTORE" (sculptor), pointing to some farmhouse.

The more expensive statuettes and other sculptures come with Chamber of Commerce certificates guaranteeing them as "entirely hand-carved." On others maybe some finishing touches were done by hand before a female employee brushed on the colors. But most of the crucifixes, Madonnas, saints, pipe-smoking peasant figures, Walt Disney characters, and wooden animals for sale were turned out by computer-steered machinery in local manufacturing plants, which may rely also on subcontractors working in their own homes. The Gherdëina wood-carving industry now not only uses local timber, but imports pricey exotic woods as well.

The valley's wood-carving enterprises market their products particularly in northern European countries and in North America; many of the multitudes of summer and winter guests also pick up some carved souvenir. The Urtijëi Art School, founded in 1872, conducts week-long wood-carving classes (three afternoon hours on Tuesday, Wednesday, and Thursday) for vacationers in July and August. During the academic year it trains local sculptors, ceramists, and painters.

A giant sample of local artistic craftsmanship is the fifteen-foot (five-meter) wooden statue of a Roman legionnaire with his helmet, shield, javelin, and sword, glowering from the corner of the Moroder wood carvings shop at 204 Streda Rezia. It was sculpted and painted by Johann Baptist Moroder in 1904 and much later covered with a film of plastic to prevent corrosion. According to an old local belief, during the barbarian invasions the remnants of a battered Roman legion found a refuge in the secluded valley, stayed on, and through several generations blended with the Rhaetian population.

❧

ON THE ALP

Urtijëi is one of the places to start a trip to the Seiser Alm/Alpe di Siusi. This is one of Europe's vastest high plateaus, unsurpassed in its panorama of the Saslonch, the Sella massif, and other Dolomite cyclops. The undulating tableland, between 5,860 and 7,136 feet (1,786 and 2,175 meters) above sea level, extends over some 20 square miles (52 square kilometers)—about the size of Manhattan. It is dotted with hundreds of hay sheds and some chalets, while a few hotels stand on its rims. Groups of spruce trees and other conifers grow here and there; little streams gurgle in deep ditches and crevices worn into the rocks through the ages; crucifixes rise on lonely paths. The colors of the grassland and of the mountain scenery all around change continually as the sun wanders and clouds sail across the sky.

The high plateau is at its most glorious, a many-colored carpet of blossoms, from May to the end of June, when the bees and butterflies are busy. Then farmers cut the grass and the flowers, lay them out to dry in the strong sun, wrap the hay into large canvases, and take the bundles to the sheds. Delicious hay smells waft about many parts of the alp. The bells of grazing cattle tinkle all summer. Strollers or hikers who set out from the edges where the access roads peter out and the hotels stand find themselves soon alone in what seems immense space. In winter the Seiser Alm/Alpe di Siusi is ideal for cross-country skiing.

The quickest means to reach the high plateau is the cableway that has its lower terminal a few hundred yards from the main square of Urtijëi. A footpath from the town across forests to the alp is steep in some stretches but presents no particular difficulties, and if you take your time, you will climb it easily in ninety minutes to two hours.

More interesting, though longer, is a hike on the road through a ravine near Bula/Pufels. This ancient Ladin hamlet is at 4,859 feet (1,481 meters) altitude, with a church that dates back to the thirteenth century and is dedicated to St. Leonhard, patron saint of cattle (a celestial rival of St. Proculus, page 100). Bula can also be reached by car over a new highway; from outside the hamlet a stony mule track across a gorge mounts to the Seiser Alm. Look at the high walls of the ravines: with their folding and wavering veins and layers of various minerals, they are a textbook of geology.

Yet other routes to the high plateau are by way of Kastelruth/Castelrotto, either from Bolzano or from Ponte Gardena/Waidbruck or from Urtijëi. From all three places good highways lead to the panoramic town, a winter and summer resort at 3,478 feet (1,060 meters) above sea level. It has a picturesque square with a fountain, old houses, a battlemented Town Hall, and a parish church with a tall steeple. Kastelruth/Castelrotto is predominantly German speaking, although its vast municipal territory includes such Ladin hamlets as Bula/Pufels.

The town faces the giant Dolomite block of the Schlern/Sciliar to its south. This craggy massif, with grassland on top and inns and refuges at various heights, has several peaks, the highest being the Petz, 8,412 feet (2,564 meters) above sea level. It commands a famous panorama of the Adige/Etsch and Isarco/

Eisack Valleys, the Rose Garden, the Marmolada and other Dolomite colossi, the Seiser Alp, and the Alpine ranges of the Austrian Tyrol.

The Schlern/Sciliar massif with a part of the Seiser Alp and the Rose Garden are within the bounds of a national park. Staked out in 1974, it extends over 25 square miles (65 square kilometers). Routes of access to it south of the Schlern: from Bolzano by way of the village of Tiers/Tires in a side valley of the Isarco River; and north of the massif from Kastelruth/Castelrotto via Völs/Fiè or Seis/Siusi and nearby places. Several chair lifts go up to the Schlern/Sciliar massif.

A specialty of the village of Völs/Fiè is its hay-bath cure. Tyrolean farmers have long treated their rheumatic ailments by burying themselves in fresh hay for half an hour or longer to bring about perspiration. When cut grass is dried and cured it produces high temperatures and is supposedly beneficial to humans. The Völser Heubad Hotel (Völs Hay Bath Hotel), with an annex, offers treatments in which patients, wrapped in large towels, are immersed in hay in a bathhouse. Some people swear by the procedure and come summer after summer for it. Allergy sufferers, however, should stay away.

Seis/Siusi, which has lent its name to the celebrated tableland, is a resort village in a magnificent location at the alp's edge and at the foot of the Schlern/Sciliar massif. A narrow road across a forest, skirting a little lake, goes to Bad Ratzes/Bagni di Razzes in a horrid ravine with iron-sulphur springs and two hotels. Oswald von Wolkenstein once went to live with his wife in a castle there but soon complained of boredom (page 179).

A good road from Seis/Siusi leads to the starting points of chair lifts up the Schlern and to the westernmost shelf of the Seiser Alp. Under pressure from environmentalists the provincial government has lately restricted the number of motor vehicles allowed on that road; its recommendation to motorists is to leave their cars at the parking areas in or near Kastelruth/Castelrotto and Seis/Siusi and to proceed by public bus or on foot.

Another, more northerly part of the Seiser Alp can be reached from Santa Cristina, some 3 miles (5 kilometers) up the Gherdëina Valley from Urtijëi. This resort village, which seems to consist entirely of hotels, inns, eating places, and carved-wood shops, groups itself at an altitude of 4,685 feet (1,428 meters) around a fifteenth-century Gothic church with a needle-roofed steeple from the thirteenth century. A chair lift and a winding road rise almost 1,000 feet (300 meters) to the Monte Pana, a ledge with a fine view of the Seiser Alp and the Dolomites on which stand the first-class Sport Hotel Monte Pana and a more modest establishment. Footpaths lead from there into the high plateau and to other chair lifts.

✍

HUNDRED-MILLION-YEAR REEF

Santa Cristina is the base from which accomplished Alpinists usually set out to measure themselves with the Long Stone, the formidable Saslonch (German: Langkofel; Italian: Sasso Lungo). This rugged rock titan, the loftiest of its prongs 10,437 feet (3,181 meters) high, is visible from many points of the Gherdëina Valley and is its most characteristic landmark. Other Dolomite peaks are higher, but the Saslonch, a hundred-million-year-old reef in what was once an ocean, represents a special challenge to rock climbers. Since the Vienna Alpinist Paul Grohmann and two Tyrolean mountain guides first scaled it in 1869, outstanding climbers explored various routes to get to the top in many hours of daring ascent, often with a bivouac on some narrow rock seam halfway up. The wild Saslonch claims its victims year after year, especially when the weather suddenly changes and snowstorms howl around the peak. A slope strewn with boulders at the foot of the redoubtable mountain is known as the Stone City; a refuge is nearby.

A little east of Santa Cristina, on the opposite side of the Gherdëina River, is the Fischburg/Castel Gardena, a towered mansion that the Wolkenstein family, lords of the valley for hundreds of years, built themselves in the seventeenth century as a summer residence and hunting lodge. The aristocrats who commissioned the project in a period of seeming quiet ordered their architect to fortify the complex with embrasures and massive walls, just in case. The mansion's German name, meaning "fish castle," alludes to trout ponds that existed nearby. A sloping forest reaches into the built-up castle area.

The oldest known seat of the Wokensteins was a small stronghold built in the thirteenth century into the mountains 3 miles (5 kilometers) northeast of Santa Cristina. Today, below a rocky overhang, a few walls survive, with empty windows and slits for shooting arrows or pouring boiling pitch on besiegers still visible. It is assumed that the minnesinger Oswald von Wolkenstein was born here if his birthplace wasn't the Trostburg above Waidbruck/Ponte Gardena (page 162).

Oswald was nine years old when one carnival night he lost his right eye, apparently because of an unfortunate stone throw or arrow shot while people were making merry and horsing around. When he was ten he ran away from home in search of adventure. He found plenty of it. According to one of his own songs, he "saw the world," at least the Mediterranean world, during fourteen years, roughing it as a stable boy, as a cook, and as an oarsman on a galley off Crete. Following the death of his father, he returned home and after a pilgrimage to the Holy Land started playing a part in Tyrolean and international politics. As a vassal of the prince-bishop of Brixen, he attended the Council of Constance, 1414–18, in which the assembled bishops attempted to assert their collective authority over the papacy. On diplomatic missions in the service of Emperor Sigismund, he toured European courts, not only conducting talks on matters of state, but also entertaining his royal hosts with his songs. His journeys took him to Morocco, where he went with the king of Portugal, and to Ireland; he claimed to have also been in Russia.

On one occasion Oswald helped detain the bishop of Brixen in a dispute between the prelate and his cathedral chapter; at other times he himself became a captive and had to buy himself out. He married a Bavarian countess and went to live with her in a castle—now a ruin—in the Hauenstein Forest near Seis (page 176) but kept hankering for more travel and excitement. With all his restlessness he lived to age seventy-eight at a time when most persons died much earlier. His tombstone near the Brixen cathedral pictures Oswald with a long beard, his right eye closed, spurred, a broadsword at his left, holding a spear.

The ruin of the original Wolkenstein Castle looks down on the village of Sëlva/Wolkenstein, which is most picturesquely situated in a little green flatland dominated by the towering cliffs of the Sella massif. The resort, at 5,141 feet (1,567 meters) above sea level, became highly fashionable with Italians when President Sandro Pertini spent his summer vacations there year after year during his tenure as head of state, 1978–85. Precious little of the

179

old village had survived by then. Today Sëlva/Wolkenstein is an agglomeration of 150 hotels, pensions, and guest houses with 5,000 beds; a dozen funiculars and chair lifts take holidaymakers to the heights.

Past the hamlet of Plan, once the terminus of the old Gherdëina railroad, the highway proceeds to the 7,264-foot (2,214-meter) Sella Pass, with the Sella to the traveler's left.

The cyclopean rock mass of the Sella, its highest point 10,338 feet (3,151 meters) above sea level, is a majestic Alpine realm by itself. Above perpendicular walls there are stony shelves and plateaus, icy clefts, a couple of little lakes that are freezing cold even on hot summer days, and fastnesses that only the chamois and the most experienced and daring climbers will scale.

The road over the Sella Pass, built during World War I for military purposes, joins the Dolomite highway, National Route 48 (page 182). A Ladin dialect is spoken in the Val di Fassa through which Route 48 runs. The area, with the towns of Moena and Canazei, belongs to the autonomous province of Trento.

Other Ladin valleys are reached by the traveler who turns left after Plan to take National Route 243, also built during World War I, to the Passo Gardena/Grödner Joch. This saddle, at an altitude of 6,959 feet (2,121 meters), is north of the Sella massif. Along rock walls that look like the ramparts of a giant fortress and across savage gorges, the highway descends in many curves into the Gadertal, also known as the Abtei Tal, or Val Badia. More than five thousand Ladins live there and in the side valleys.

The villages of the upper Val Badia/Gadertal—Kolfusch/Colfosco, Corvara, La Villa/Stern, St. Cassian, Pedraces, and St. Leonhard/San Leonardo—are much-frequented winter and summer resorts. The broadening valley, almost a high plateau at 4,500–5,400 feet (1,370–1,640 meters) above sea level, is enclosed by high rock bastions. Some tight clusters of Ladin farmsteads on the slopes, caled *viles* (hamlets) in the local idiom, have been given landmark status. Hotels, inns, furnished apartments and rooms for rent, eating places, sports installations, and chair lifts are plentiful; two dozen mountain refuges dot the nearby slopes and summits.

St. Vigil/San Vigilio (Ladin: Plan de Mareo) in the lateral Enneberg/Marebbe Valley, not quite 12 miles (18 kilometers) by highway south of Bruneck/Brunico, is particularly popular with winter sports enthusiasts. It lies in a vast bowl at an altitude of 3,940 feet (1,201 meters), surrounded by attractive slopes with long pistes; the Dolomites to the south provide a dramatic backdrop. In the summer months many guests of the village undertake hikes and mountain tours on a variety of marked paths and tracks.

A larger-than-life statue of Catarina Lanz, the "Maid of Spinges" (page 140), holding her pitchfork, was unveiled in St. Vigil in 1971 on the two-hundredth anniversary of the Ladin heroine's birth.

The lower part of the Gadertal/Val Badia, before the torrent joins the Rienza River, is a gorge; the road, National Route 244, is narrow and snakelike in some stretches.

VIII.

PALLID AND
PURPLE GIANTS

❧

K ing Laurin's magic realm of pallid mountains that turn pink
and purple in the glow of the rising and setting sun, when
the valleys are still or enveloped in dusk, is the most sensational
district of the Alps; many consider it the grandest landscape on
the Continent.

Long secluded and even shunned, the awe-inspiring Dolomites began attracting foreign visitors only in the second half of
the nineteenth century. Today the most impressive route for
penetrating the unique domain of jagged mountains is the Great
Dolomite Road from Bolzano to the "Queen of the Dolomites,"
Cortina d'Ampezzo.

The highway, one of Italy's outstanding sights, is 68 miles
(109 kilometers) long. It was built, principally for military reasons,
by Austria-Hungary between the second half of the nineteenth
century and the first years of World War I across wild gorges
and over three major mountain passes where only footpaths and
mule tracks existed before. Under Italian administration the highway—National Routes 241 and 48—was greatly improved. It is
today much traveled by sight-seeing coaches and other tourist
vehicles.

The first section of the Great Dolomite Road traverses the

Eggental/Valle d'Ega, which opens to the Eisack/Isarco River at a point 2 miles (about 3 kilometers) east of Bolzano's center, near the Bolzano North exit of the Brenner motorway, A-22, and opposite the Bolzano hydroelectric plant. The massive Karneid/Cornedo Castle, a thirteenth-century fortress with a square donjon on top of a 550-foot (168-meter) rock, overlooks from the north the ravine that is the entrance to the side valley.

The reddish porphyry walls of the gorge almost touch each other at some points. The road passes a cascade over a bridge and a tunnel, reaching Birchabruck/Pontenova, 2,877 feet (877 meters) above sea level, where the valley broadens, offering splendid vistas of the Rose Garden to the left (north) and the Latemar to the right. Mount Latemar is a rugged group of gray rock whose highest pinnacle is at an altitude of 9,337 feet (2,846 meters), visible from Bolzano.

From Birchabruck/Pontenova a provincial road, turning south, leads to the little village of Deutschnofen/Nova Ponente and, at a little distance, to the shrine of Maria Weissenstein/ Madonna di Montalba. This seventeenth-century church, incorporating a sixteenth-century chapel, at 4,990 feet (1,521 meters) above sea level, is the most revered pilgrimage center in South Tyrol. Countless devotees, also from the Trentino, have walked to it, usually in a couple of hours across the woods from Leifers/ Laives, a village on the Adige that today is a virtual suburb of Bolzano.

The pilgrimage church, of undistinguished architecture with a squat tower and two front turrets, contains a marble statue of the Virgin Mary and numerous votive tablets expressing gratitude to the Madonna for supposed miraculous cures and mercies. Pope John Paul II visited the shrine in July 1988 and, speaking in

German, Italian, and Ladin, addressed the crowd that had gathered that day.

⟋⟍

MOUNTAIN-WAR MEMORIES

Following Route 241 through dense spruce and pine forests, the traveler passes the village of Welschnofen/Nova Levante, which is hemmed in by wooded slopes and serves as the starting point for most mountain tours into the Rose Garden group. Many guests of the three dozen hotels and inns in and near the village also come for the Karersee/Lago di Carezza at 5,279 feet (1,609 meters) above sea level, a lake as famous as the Pragser Wildsee/ Lago di Braies in a side valley of the Pustertal (page 147). A forest path known as the Elisabeth Promenade leads in a little more than an hour's walking from Welschnofen to the little lake. Its bottle-green, clear water mirrors the spruce trees densely surrounding it and the rocky spires (the "Dolls") of the Latemar's crest in the south. Empress Elisabeth of Austria-Hungary loved the scenery and often wandered to the lake. Cableways and chair lifts go up to the Rose Garden and Latemar heights from points nearby.

East of the lake, Route 241 climbs to the Karer Pass/Passo di Costalunga, which at an altitude of 5,751 feet (1,753 meters) marks the border between the autonomous provinces of Bolzano/ Südtirol and Trento. The highway descends to the Ladin-speaking Fassa Valley, disclosing grandiose vistas of the Sella massif to the north and of the Marmolada, the highest complex of the Dolomites, straight ahead.

Near the village of Vigo di Fassa, Route 241 joins the highway linking Trento with Cortina d'Ampezzo, Route 48; it branches off the old Brenner Road and Motorway A-22 at Auer/Ora, 11 miles (18 kilometers) south of Bolzano. The first Ladin settlement along Route 48, 6.5 miles (10.5 kilometers) from the Auer/Ora turnoff, is Moena, a winter and summer resort.

Eight miles (13 kilometers) north of Vigo di Fassa is the principal tourist center of the Fassa Valley, Canazei, at 4,806 feet (1,465 meters) above sea level. Picturesquely situated in a little bowl girded by forested slopes, with a panorama of Dolomite walls and summits, the town with its many hotels and pensions is the natural base for ascents of the Marmolada group.

The Marmolada is the most compact, vast, and lofty of all Dolomite mountains; the highest of its several peaks rises to 10,965 feet (3,342 meters) above sea level. The Marmolada glacier on the group's north slope is the largest in the entire Dolomite district.

The southern side of the mountain complex descends almost vertically as a giant, craggy wall to the valley of the Ombretta torrent. Crack mountain climbers have conquered the Marmolada's fearful south wall over various routes across patches with overhanging rocks in twelve to eighteen hours.

During World War I mountain troops of Austria-Hungary and Italy faced each other for three years on the Marmolada, firing at each other with howitzers and mortars, tunneling through ice and rock, digging grottoes and trenches into the flanks of the massif, descending by rope on enemy positions in daring surprise assaults, and blowing up each other's strongholds by burrowing below them and planting tremendous mines. Many remains of the high-altitude front lines can still be seen; old military roads and tracks crisscross the Marmolada district.

Today summer tourists wearing running shoes, some accompanied by children, nonchalantly ascend the summit of the Marmolada group by a system of cableways starting from the hamlet of Malga Ciapela on the south side of the massif. It is reached from Canazei on a good road across forests and over the Fedaia Pass at an altitude of 6,749 feet (2,057 meters), near an artificial lake storing glacier and snow water for a power plant.

From Canazei, in a sequence of large curves amid a spruce forest, Route 48 mounts to a shelf with hotels and chair lifts, where it then forks. To the north, the Sella Pass Road (page 180) provides communication with the Gherdëina Valley and Ladinia; Route 48 continues in another series of steep bends to the Pordoi Pass, 7,346 feet (2,239 meters) above sea level. The Pordoi is a grassy saddle with hotels, a mountaineers' hostel, and a magnificent panorama. To the south the Marmolada with its glacier is visible; the Rose Garden is in the west, the Sella massif and Saslonch are in the north, and the Dolomite mountains surrounding Cortina d'Ampezzo can be seen in the east. A cableway and a chair lift go up to the Sella from the pass. An obelisk on its south side carries a bronze tablet recording the completion of the highway in 1909.

Descending from the Pordoi Pass in large bends across pastures, the traveler enters the Veneto region and the province of Belluno. Route 48 passes the village of Arabba, which was completely destroyed during World War I with the exception of the seventeenth-century parish church. Route 244 turns off into the Val Badia/Gadertal (page 180) toward Corvara. A little more than 4 miles (7 kilometers) farther along Route 48 is the village of Pieve di Livinallongo/Buchenstein, which is Ladin and also suffered heavily during World War I.

Mountain-war buffs set out from here to visit the legendary Col di Lana, which is 8,077 feet (2,462 meters) high. It saw furious fighting between 1915 and 1917, when it was several times lost and reconquered by the forces of Austria-Hungary and Italy at a monstrous cost of human lives on either side. In April 1916 Italian engineers, who had for months been tunneling in the rock, blew up the summit of the mountain with several tons of the most powerful explosive then known. Military galleries and enormous blast holes caused by the mines and countermines that either side had sprung convey a chilling idea of the ferocity of the battles at the unprecedented altitude of 1.5 miles (nearly 2.5 kilometers) above sea level. A chapel that was built on top of what had remained of the Col di Lana after the war commemorates the soldiers who died on the mountain. Military cemeteries and war memorials dot a wide area. Talk to any local residents today and they will all shake their heads about the madness of a war that brought immense suffering to their villages.

From Pieve di Livinallongo/Buchenstein Route 48 skirts the Col di Lana and passes the ruin of Andraz Castle on an isolated rock spur. The stronghold, dating from the eleventh century, once belonged to the bishops of Brixen; Nicolaus Cusanus at one time found a refuge in it when the henchmen of Duke Sigismund of Tyrol were after him. The road rises in large curves and through a tunnel to the Falzárego Pass, at an altitude of 6,906 feet (2,105 meters). The Falzárego is a wide gap strewn with boulders between stone walls.

*

ADVENTURER AND SCIENTIST

The final section of the Great Dolomite Road—10 miles (16 kilometers) from the Falzárego Pass to Cortina d'Ampezzo—is spectacular. As the road descends across pastures and forests, the enormous cliffs of the rugged Tófane become visible on one's left. The Tófane are a group of three mighty peaks, the middle and highest Tófana rising to 10,640 feet (3,243 meters) altitude. The highway turns north in curves around Mount Pocol and goes down into the vast, sunny basin of Cortina d'Ampezzo. That rolling plain is surrounded by an incomparable amphitheater of Dolomite towers, spires, pillars, and rock bastions.

Route 48 approaches the city of Cortina d'Ampezzo from its northern suburbs and crosses the Bóite torrent, which skirts it on its west side, running southward to join the Piave River.

Near the Olympic Stadium on the northern outskirts of Cortina d'Ampezzo, on the east bank of the torrent, is a large triangular chunk of rock with a bronze relief portrait of the Frenchman who gave his name to a special kind of mineral and to the entire Alpine district where it occurs—Dieudonné (said Déodat) Guy Sylvain Tancrède de Gratet of the counts of Dolomieu (1750–1801). The monument was erected at French insistence in 1958.

Dolomieu was one of the many cosmopolitan adventurers that the Rococo age brought forth, and as a self-taught geologist he became a pioneer of science. He was the ninth son of a nobleman in the village of Dolomieu, about halfway between Lyon and Grenoble, which he left at the age of nine. He later enlisted in the Order of Malta, then a sovereign power, and when he was eighteen took service on one of its galleys. In the seaport of Gaeta, north of Naples, he killed a fellow officer in a duel and was arrested, shipped back to Malta, and sentenced to death. Pope Clement XIII interceded on his behalf, and Dolomieu was released from prison at La Valletta, the island capital, after nine months. He returned to France, where he did some military service, and eventually left the king's army to devote himself to the study of mineralogy.

In his thirties Dolomieu toured France, Spain, Portugal, Morocco, and Italy, visiting mines, mountain sites, and islands. In July 1787 he observed an eruption of Mount Etna in Sicily; he reached the conclusion that volcanic activity and earthquakes were related. Between 1788 and 1790, while the French Revolution broke out and shook his native country, Dolomieu was studying the Alpine rock formations that would be named after him. Examining the mineral samples that he collected, he found that their mixture of calcium and magnesium carbonate was special, harder than the limestone that is diffuse in the Alps. He announced his discovery in one of his several writings, and Nicolas de Saussure—a son of the Swiss physician and mineralogist who was among the first persons to climb to the highest summit of the Alps, Mont Blanc—proposed to call that particular rock from the "pale mountains" Dolomie.

On his return to France, Dolomieu supported the Revolution as a moderate. In 1798 he joined General Bonaparte's expedition to Egypt together with other scientists, hoping to have chances for examining African geological phenomena. Napoleon, however, sent the former Knight of Malta to La Valletta to negotiate the island power's surrender. Dolomieu did make it to Egypt eventually but wasn't able to do much scientific research there. On his way back he was shipwrecked, was captured by the police of the Bourbon king of Naples, and spent twenty-one months in fetid southern Italian jails. As a prisoner he wrote his most important work, *Mineralogical Philosophy*, scribbling on strips of cloth and on the margins of a Bible, the only book allowed him. Napoleon at long last obtained his liberation. Dolomieu died shortly after his return home.

The only existing portrait of Dolomieu, now in the Grenoble regional museum, is by Angelica Kauffmann, the Swiss painter who was a protegée of Sir Joshua Reynolds and a friend of Goethe and other celebrities. She pictured the scientist with a high forehead, a prominent nose, and friendly eyes. Contemporaries described Dolomieu as a tall and usually stooping person, proud to the point of arrogance, and a redoubtable ladies' man.

Geologists assume today that the material making up much of the Dolomites was formed in the Triassic era, beginning two hundred million years ago, when the area was covered by Tethys, a central ocean. Many fossils of marine organisms found in the "pallid mountains" indeed prove the sedimentary nature of their rocks—reefs and atolls grown through the aeons. Volcanic matter is intermingled. In younger geological eras immense telluric forces are supposed to have pushed the Triassic layers north, folding them into high mountain systems. During the Ice Ages enormous glaciers dug valleys and rounded peaks and ranges. The eroding action of ice, water, sun, wind, snow, and rain is thought to have played a key role in the creation of the fantastic shapes of the Dolomites.

ༀ

DESIGNER LABELS

The Ampezzo Valley through which the Bóite torrent flows, and especially the Cortina basin, seem to have been inhabited, if only sparsely, in ancient Roman times. Domination by the Langobards or Lombards during the early Middle Ages left the peasants and cattle breeders of the Ampezzo district with a body of community rules, the *regulae*, that covered property rights such as the use of pastures, forests, and water; these regulations were observed until modern times. The Ampezzo dialect is related to Ladin and close to the idiom spoken in the remainder of the Friuli region.

In the late Middle Ages the Ampezzo district passed from rule by the counts of Tyrol to that of the Republic of Venice. Between 1511 and World War I the area was a part of the Austrian Tyrol, except for a few years during the Napoleonic era. The population kept clinging to the ancient Ampezzo "rules" and asserting its old privileges. To be a native of the Ampezzo district and possibly descend from generations of local farmers is a matter of considerable pride.

The traditional costumes of the Ampezzo Valley betray influences from both the Tyrol and Venice. On festive occasions the women wear gaudy aprons over long black skirts, white long-sleeved shirts with embroideries and frills, tight bodices in brilliant colors, fringed kerchiefs, and graceful hats adorned with ribbons and filigree pins—essentially a southern attire. The men, on the other hand, look Tyrolean in their brown loden and leather outfits.

Mountain climbers started defying the Dolomite peaks around 1860, a few years after most of the highest tops in the French and Swiss Alps had been conquered. During the following decades British, Austrian, German, and Belgian rock climbers flocked to Cortina d'Ampezzo to scale the mountains around the town. Local mountaineers served as guides, developing an enduring tradition of reliable professionalism; the Association of Ampezzo Guides is to this day a highly respected group. The completion of the Great Dolomite Road from Auer/Ora to Cortina d'Ampezzo in 1909 brought many new foreign visitors.

The first hotels were opened in Cortina d'Ampezzo in 1875. By 1910 the town still counted only a few hundred permanent residents but was well equipped to accommodate an increasing number of guests. World War I put a stop to the promising tourist business; the hotels and pensions had to house military staffs or serve as hospitals. Italian forces occupied Cortina d'Ampezzo without much fighting in May 1915 while the Austrians took up positions in the nearby mountains. The Italians abandoned the town in November 1917, when an enemy offensive forced them to take back their front lines to the Piave River. The Austrians reoccupied Cortina d'Ampezzo, only to hand it back to the Italians in 1918 following the collapse of the Hapsburg monarchy. Cortina d'Ampezzo suffered very little damage during World War I: there was a tacit agreement to spare the town.

The hotels of Cortina d'Ampezzo were reconverted to civilian use; guests from foreign countries and other provinces of Italy started filling them again in the summer months. One frequent visitor of the Dolomites was Albert, king of the Belgians, a mountaineering enthusiast. He was to die in a rock-climbing accident— not in his beloved "pale mountains," but at home near Namur in 1934. A bust placed on a block of Dolomite rock near the Corona Bridge at the center of Cortina d'Ampezzo commemorates the royal Alpinist. During the 1920s, but especially after World War II, Cortina d'Ampezzo developed into one of Italy's top winter sports centers and became citified.

Today the air of Cortina d'Ampezzo, at 4,016 feet (1,224 meters) above sea level, is still invigorating despite exhaust fumes; the sunshine is generous in winter and summer; and the panorama remains unique. Yet the city has changed its character since around 1950. At present it is not just a headquarters for mountaineering and skiing, but also—and above all—has become an elegant resort where many of its trendy guests content themselves with looking from below at the summits and ski runs.

The core of Cortina has expanded and now looks thoroughly urban with condominiums, supermarkets, boutiques, fine restaurants, neon-lit espresso bars, and nightclubs. Chalet-type second homes of well-to-do people from Milan, Turin, Venice, Bologna, Rome, and other Italian cities, quite a few of them show business and media personalities, have sprouted on the outskirts. In 1994 an apartment in a prime location cost $700 per square foot (about $7,500 per square meter), the highest price in any northern Italian resort, comparable only to what an apartment on Venice's Grand Canal might cost.

Cortina d'Ampezzo has today a resident population of 7,500; thousands more seem to feel they just have to make an appearance during the Christmas and Easter vacations and in August. Cappuccino in the morning and predinner aperitif at the bar of the Hôtel de la Poste at the city center are as much a compelling ritual as is strolling up and down the Corso d'Italia in the late afternoon. Pseudo-Alpine designer fashions are the correct dress the same way as the many new villas imitate the traditional Alpine houses—broad fronts with wooden balconies and wooden gables under sloping roofs—while interiors are styled by renowned designers. To many winter guests après-ski in the night spots is far more important than schussing down the superb pistes in the vicinity.

Joggers work out in the morning on a gently curving promenade that is the former roadbed of the long defunct Dolomites railroad from Toblach/Dobbiaco to Calalzo di Cadore. The Olympic Ice Stadium and other sports facilities in and around Cortina d'Ampezzo are in part a legacy from the 1956 Olympic Winter Games. Twenty-five years later, however, the town declined the honor of playing host to another edition of the global winter sports event. Although the hotel and catering industries understandably advocated a bid for another Cortina d'Ampezzo Winter Olympics, a majority of residents found that the inevitable congestion and other ecological woes would be too much trouble.

✒

CHALETS AND CHAMOIS

The architectural symbol of Cortina d'Ampezzo is the detached, square tower of the parish Church of Saints Philip and James at the very middle of the city. The steeple, built from 1853 to 1858 with white stones from nearby quarries, is 249 feet (76 meters) high and is topped by a hexagonal crown carrying a short green dome with a gilt sphere and a cross. A circular gallery above the bell loft commands an overwhelming, nearly 360-degree panorama. Metal tablets on the parapet indicate the mountains surrounding the Ampezzo basin that can be seen, giving their altitudes. The solemn and harmonious peals of the six bells, when tolled in unison, are heard all over the highlands.

The parish church is older than its belfry. It was built in the Baroque style in 1773 on the site of an earlier edifice and has attractive ceiling frescoes as well as, on the first side altar on the left, an eighteenth-century tabernacle in richly carved wood.

A small church in the south of the city, known as the Madonna della Difesa (Our Lady of the Defense), dates from the sixteenth century and was rebuilt in 1743. Its name alludes to a legend of a miraculous intercession by the Virgin Mary to save the early-medieval town from being looted and razed by the Langobard conquerors. The town cemetery is nearby.

Another Cortina d'Ampezzo sight is the so-called Picture Palace, a frescoed private house of no particular architectural distinction at the north end of the Corso d'Italia. Three artistic brothers of the local Ghedina family decorated the building's outer walls toward the end of the nineteenth century with murals representing the Ages of Man, the Muses, and, above the entrance door, the national hero Giuseppe Garibaldi. The Picture Palace has officially been designated as a landmark.

The Civic Museum, 17 Corso d'Italia, occupies a part of the seventeenth-century Ciasa de Ra Regoles (House of the Ampezzo Rules), which is also the repository of the Ampezzo Archives. The museum contains a fossil collection, products of local arts and handicrafts, and works by twentieth-century artists who were not or were only loosely connected with the region, including paintings by Giorgio de Chirico and Giorgio Morandi. Scholars may consult ancient documents concerning the Ampezzo community in the archives.

The center of Cortina d'Ampezzo is surrounded by hotels with parks, swimming pools, and tennis courts; by clusters of chalets; and by much older hamlets and villages, called *ra viles* in the local idiom. The ancient houses in the hamlets cling together and often look in the same direction, southeast or southwest, according to their location in the Ampezzo basin, in order to get most of the sunshine.

Some of the hamlets, like Gillardon to the west of the city or nearby Lacedel, have become fashionable because of posh restaurants with magnificent views. Other favorite excursion and eating spots are the little Lake Ghedina at an altitude of 4,754 feet (1,449 meters) northwest of the city and the Pocol Belvedere, 5,049 feet (1,539 meters) above sea level, not quite 4 miles (6 kilometers) southwest of Cortina d'Ampezzo's center and linked with it by bus service. The Pocol Belvedere affords a stunning panorama; nearby is an ossuary, a 157-foot (48-meter) square tower containing the remains of 7,500 World War I soldiers, most of them disinterred from the district's military cemeteries.

From points near Cortina d'Ampezzo funiculars take passengers up to the middle peak (the highest of the three) of the Tófane group and to the ski slopes of the Faloria Alp to the east, some 3,000 feet (nearly 1,000 meters) above the city. There is a multitude of ski lifts to choose from in the environs.

Ecological groups like Mountain Wilderness have lately opposed projects for further development in the heart of the Dolomites, such as more funiculars. As for mountaineering, almost all possible routes to the summits by way of rock walls, slabs, chimneys, couloirs, and overhangs seem to have been thoroughly explored and mapped and all peaks, ridges, and spires conquered. The approaches to the Dolomite ramparts are dotted with hotels, inns, and refuges. Steel spikes left in the rocks by pioneer climbers, and permanent passages with spikes, metal steps, and ropes on some much frequented climbing routes, assist less daring mountaineers. A new school of freeclimbers disdains such aids.

The possibilities for excursions from Cortina d'Ampezzo by car, cableway, or chair lift, and for hikes and climbs, are dazzling. On the slopes one may still have a fleeting encounter with deer, at least at some distance. Only in winter when the timid animals are hungry will they come out of the evergreen woods to the places where the forest service or farmers strew feed for them.

The rocks above the treeline are the windy habitat of the chamois, who live off the grass and low brushes growing on the heights. From various vantage points, through binoculars, I have over the years observed isolated chamois—apparently males— and little herds and admired the insouciance with which the animals were grazing on giddying heights, suddenly interrupting their meal with bizarre leaps to some distant rock. I have never seen an ibex in the Dolomites, although a few of the long-horned wild goats are known to be around still; the species is protected by law. Marmots can be seen fairly often, and eagles wheel high above the peaks every now and then.

During the early 1990s footprints and other sightings indicated that a few brown bears had immigrated from the east into the Italian Dolomites and had reached places only 20 miles (30 kilometers) from Cortina d'Ampezzo. The animals are supposed to have come from the woodlands of Croatia and Slovenia, slowly foraging westward across the least accessible forested slopes of Carinthia. The last bear in the Dolomites was killed near the Ampezzo Valley in 1830; local environmentalists were highly pleased that plantigrades from the Balkans might again be colonizing their region.

At the beginning of the 1990s half a dozen brown bears were also still living in the forests of the wild Brenta Dolomites of Trento Province near the resort of Madonna di Campiglio; they were under official protection as an endangered species, and there were plans to import a few more bears from other European countries and set them free in the mountains of the upper Brenta.

✺

TITIAN'S COUNTRY

Cortina d'Ampezzo is a crossroads where two important Alpine highways meet. The Great Dolomite Road intersects here with National Route 51, a link in a transportation system from Venice to the Pustertal/Val Pusteria and onward to Austria and Germany. Since the early nineteenth century, when the north-south road across the Dolomites by way of Cortina d'Ampezzo was completed, it was known as the Strada d'Alemagna, or Germany Highway. The Green lobby has fiercely opposed a recent plan to build a motor road version of the Strada d'Alemagna, more or less parallel to Route 51, in order to create a Munich–Venice expressway via Cortina d'Ampezzo. Only the southernmost section of the project has been completed; as Motorway A-27 it runs from a point north of Venice to the town of Vittorio Veneto (where the Austrian-Hungarian forces were decisively beaten by Italian and Allied divisions in 1918) and another 16 miles (26 kilometers) northward to the village of Pian di Vedoia.

Driving down the valley of the Bóite torrent from Cortina d'Ampezzo, the traveler comes to the picturesque district of the Cadore, the upper Piave Valley. The town of Pieve di Cadore, on an artificial lake 19 miles (30 kilometers) southeast of Cortina d'Ampezzo, is worth a visit not only as the birthplace of Titian, but also because of its pretty location high above the young Piave River. (The name *Pieve di Cadore* has nothing to do with the river. *Pieve* is an Italian term denoting a major parish church with jurisdiction over local chapels.)

A bronze statue of the great native son stands in the town's main square. Tiziano Vecelli was born in 1477 (or 1488, or 1489) as a son of a local notable who had been a military man. As a young boy he was sent by his parents to an uncle in Venice and became an apprentice to the Bellini painter brothers, Gentile and Giovanni; eventually he entered an artistic partnership with the formidable Giorgione. A highly prolific artist, Titian soon won fame all over Europe. He portrayed Emperor Charles V, who made him a count palatine; in Rome he painted Pope Paul III with his grandsons, earning the Vatican's knighthood of the Golden Spur (which more than two hundred years later would also be bestowed on the young Mozart).

Titian became very rich and obtained for his father in Pieve di Cadore the lucrative job of inspector of mines. The master often represented the Cadore mountains in his paintings and as an old man returned to his native town to decorate its church (his frescoes have long been detached and are now in Venice). Titian was in his late eighties or nineties (depending on when he was actually born) when he died during a plague epidemic in Venice in 1576. Enveloped in the cloak of a count palatine, he was buried in the Church of Santa Maria Gloriosa dei Frari in Venice, where his celebrated *Assumption* adorns the high altar.

Pieve di Cadore has a distinctive Venetian flavor. The house in which Titian was born is on the intimate Piazza della Fontana; the building includes a small museum where letters written by the artist, his 1533 patent of nobility, and other memorabilia are shown. The only painting by Titian in all of Pieve di Cadore is in the third side chapel on the left of the parish church, picturing the Virgin Mary between two saints (the figure on the left of the Madonna is assumed to be a self-portrait by the master). The Museum of the Cadore in a Renaissance building on the main square, Piazza Tiziano, contains archaeological material and documents from the period between the fifteenth and eighteenth centuries when the upper Piave Valley formed a semiautonomous district of the Republic of Venice.

A few miles to the north, close to the elongated Lake of Pieve di Cadore, is the village of Calalzo di Cadore, with the terminal of the railroad line from Venice and Padua. Passengers arriving by train at the station of Calalzo-Pieve di Cadore can transfer to buses taking them to Cortina d'Ampezzo in about an hour.

Driving southward on the west bank of the Piave on Route 51 and then on Route 50 for a total of 26 miles (41 kilometers), one reaches Belluno, the capital of the province that includes Cortina d'Ampezzo and a large sector of the Dolomites. The city of some forty thousand population at the confluence of the Piave and Ardo Rivers has an impressive square with old palaces in front of a sixteenth-century cathedral with a 217-foot (66-meter) Venetian-style campanile. The Civic Museum at 16 Piazza del Duomo displays excavations and a collection of paintings and sculptures, principally by Venetian artists.

Pope John Paul I, the former Albino Luciani, who was head of the Roman Catholic Church for only thirty-four days in 1978 and was the first pontiff in history who chose a double name for himself, was born in 1912 in the small village of Forno di Canale, 3,202 feet (976 meters) high, about 30 miles (48 kilometers) northwest of Belluno and at about the same distance from Cortina d'Ampezzo. The Dolomite pope was cardinal-patriarch of Venice before his elevation to the throne of St. Peter.

I have explored many of the Dolomite highways north of Belluno by car at various times because as a boy I had heard my father speak so much about them and their hairpin bends. During World War I he ferried ammunition to the front lines on unpaved military roads as an Austrian army corporal in charge of four supply trucks that had steel wheels instead of rubber tires. They frequently drove under Italian artillery fire, and Father said he was always prepared for some shell to hit his truck and blow him up with his urgently needed ammunition, but none did.

To tell the truth, as a child I was soon bored by my father's war recollections—he had just been doing his job, hadn't he? He had no heroic feats to tell. Only many years later, after I had myself experienced the long tedium and sudden terrors of military operations, did I realize what a rotten time Father must have had in that setting of surpassing natural beauty.

National Route 51, mounting the Piave Valley, is the southern gateway to the Dolomites. The northern access, as mentioned on page 149, is Route 51 between Toblach/Dobbiaco and Cortina d'Ampezzo. Between Schluderbach/Carbonin, where Gustav Mahler spent his working vacations, and the Queen of the Dolomites, the traveler has two options.

The 12 miles (18.5 kilometers) of Route 51 traverse a grandiose Dolomite landscape. To the east are the mighty precipices of Mount Cristallo, which is 10,551 feet (3,216 meters) high and in part covered with a glacier. On the west, the Fanes Valley opens toward the Bóite torrent. That side valley leads into one of the most solitary parts of the Dolomites, with bizarrely shaped mountains, rock shelves strewn with boulders, little lakes, cascades, and sparse forests. Ladin folk tales tell of a brilliant, rich mountain kingdom that once had its center in the Fanes Alp and Valley; today the loneliness of the rocky core of the Dolomites hardly suggests any splendid past.

The highway between Cortina d'Ampezzo and Schluderbach/Carbonin described above follows the roadbed of the former Dolomite railroad. Most tourists today take instead National Route 48 bis (*bis* is Latin for twice and in Italian usage indicates a variant). The scenic highway is 15 miles (24 kilometers) long and passes the beautiful Lake Misurina. The Passo Tre Croci (Three Crosses Pass), 5.5 miles (nearly 9 kilometers) northeast of Cortina d'Ampezzo, 5,935 feet (1,809 meters) above sea level, commands a splendid view of the huge Tófane group, with the ominous Col di Lana of World War I notoriety to the left of it. Farther south, the snow-covered peaks of the Marmolada are visible; to the north, Mount Cristallo dominates the panorama. The lower terminus of a cableway leading up Mount Cristallo is a little below the pass.

Lake Misurina, 9 miles (15 kilometers) northeast of Cortina d'Ampezzo and 4.5 miles (7 kilometers) from Schluderbach/Carbonin, is an elongated expanse of ice-green water surrounded by clumps of conifers and jagged mountains. King Albert of the Belgians was a frequent guest in one of the hotels looking out on the lake and the Dolomites. A pleasant walk around the shores in the bracing air of 5,758 feet (1,755 meters) above sea level takes an hour or so.

IX.

MOUNTAIN MEMO:
PRACTICAL
INFORMATION

❧

GETTING THERE   The quickest way to reach the sunny side of the Alps from the Western Hemisphere or Britain is by air to Innsbruck, Milan, Venice, or Verona, proceeding by railroad or car. Innsbruck and Verona, both connected with international aviation hubs by feeder airlines, are closest to the region. Bolzano/ Bozen, the capital of South Tyrol, is a one-hour train ride distant from Verona; travel to Bolzano from Innsbruck takes a little more than two hours, including formalities at the Austrian-Italian border on the Brenner Pass.

Venice Airport is particularly convenient for visits to the Dolomites. The car trip from Mestre on the mainland near Venice's Marco Polo Airport to Cortina d'Ampezzo, the main center of the Dolomites, on Motorway A-4 and Motorway A-27, proceeding on National Route 51, takes about two hours. Travel by train from Venice or Padua to Calalzo di Cadore, proceeding by public bus to Cortina d'Ampezzo, lasts four hours. A trip on the scenic Dolomites Road from Bolzano to Cortina d'Ampezzo involves a car or bus ride of two to three hours.

PUBLIC TRANSPORTATION   The line from Verona to Trento, Bolzano, Bressanone/Brixen, the Brenner Pass, and

Innsbruck is a main route of the European railroad network, handling international and express trains, local passenger services, and a large volume of freight traffic. Frequent trains on the Bolzano–Merano line link the two biggest cities in South Tyrol in thirty to forty minutes, depending on intermediate stops. Another railroad line branches off the Brenner route at Fortezza/Franzensfeste, runs the length of the Val Pusteria/Pustertal, connects with buses to Cortina d'Ampezzo at Toblach/Dobbiaco, and east of San Candido/Innichen ties in with the railroad network of Austria's East Tyrol and Carinthia.

A system of buses provides service to all towns as well as most villages of interest, reaching also into many side valleys of the region. The integrated bus network comprises the semipublic SAD (Servizi Autobus Dolomiti/Südtiroler Autobus Dienst) and private enterprises. Schedules are available at the bus terminal at Perathoner-Strasse in Bolzano near the city's railroad station and in all tourist offices in the area. Buy bus tickets at counters near major stops or from the driver. No round-trip tickets are issued, but if you keep your one-way ticket and show it on a same-day return trip, you get a discount.

Car Travel   The main highway axis in the Trentino and South Tyrol is the toll Motorway A-22 from Modena to Verona, Rovereto, Trento, Bolzano/Bozen, Bressanone/Brixen, and the Brenner Pass, continuing in the Austrian Tyrol as A-13 to Innsbruck (also a toll road). The A-22 autostrada is more or less parallel to the old Brenner Road, S.S. 12, which continues from the Brenner Pass to Innsbruck as B 182. (S.S. stands for *strada statale*, or national route; B, in Austria, stands for *Bundesstrasse*, or federal highway.)

Quite a few motorists prefer to travel on S.S. 12 and B 182, not only to save motorway tolls, but also because the old, narrow highway is scenic during long stretches and gives a better feel of the landscape and the towns and villages it touches than does the autostrada and its Austrian counterpart. Motorway A-27 branches off the Milan–Venice motorway, A-4, north of Mestre and runs for some 40 miles (64 kilometers) northward in the direction of the Dolomites, proceeding to Cortina d'Ampezzo as S.S. 51. An old project to build a motorway across the Dolomites area and along the Val Pusteria/Pustertal to create a Venice–Munich expressway has been halted by strong opposition from environmentalists.

South Tyrol, the Trentino, and the Dolomites are crisscrossed by several other national highways. They are marked by the letters *S.S.* and a number. In addition to the national routes there are many local roads topped with asphalt, concrete, or macadam. Lately the autonomous province of Bolzano/Südtirol has taken on responsibility for several highways that up to then were classified as national routes.

For traveling on mountain roads, a car with a stick shift is preferable to one with an automatic gearshift because the former gives the driver better control in the frequent curves and on steep grades. Be wary of cars on the road carrying BZ (Bolzano), TN (Trento), or BL (Belluno) license plates: local drivers are of course familiar with the highways and traffic patterns, but many of them seem overconfident, drive too fast for safety, take reckless chances, and tend to tailgate. The two letters on Italian license plates identifying the province where the vehicle is registered are being phased out so that in the future it won't be possible to tell a car's provenance at a glance. If you spot an aggressive driver in your rear mirror on a winding Alpine road, pull aside and let the daredevil pass.

Cabs can be summoned by phone anywhere throughout

the region. Consult the bilingual Bolzano/Südtirol telephone directory or the directories for the provinces of Trento or Belluno under the heading Taxi. Cab ranks exist in Bolzano, Merano, Bressanone, and other major towns. If you want to hire a taxi for a sight-seeing tour or some other longer trip, agree with the driver on the fare beforehand. A half-day excursion by cab from Bolzano to Cortina d'Ampezzo on the Dolomite Road may cost $250; it is customary to treat the driver to a snack on such a tour.

Coach trips to major sights in the region and to more distant destinations like Venice, Lake Garda, or Innsbruck are conducted by SAD (page 204) and by other travel organizations with offices in all the major towns.

HIKING AND TREKKING   For generations hiking has been popular in South Tyrol and in the Dolomites from spring to late autumn. The region's national parks and nature reservations as well as other areas for exploring the landscape on foot or mountain bike are described in chapters 3 through 8. Advice and information may be obtained from the provincial tourism agencies (page 216). Bookshops and many news vendors throughout the region offer a vast selection of hiking maps. Principal paths for hikers are marked everywhere.

Camping sites may be found all over South Tyrol, the Trentino, and the Dolomites; some of these are in operation all year. For listings and fees, contact the provincial tourism agencies.

MOUNTAINEERING   The sheer rock walls of the Dolomites are a university of Alpinism. Other peaks, ranges, massifs, and slopes throughout the region present challenges of every degree of difficulty to mountain climbers. Alpinism schools in the area's towns and resorts conduct climbing classes and mountain tours; licensed mountain guides can be hired in Cortina d'Ampezzo and in many localities in South Tyrol and the Trentino. Several chapters of the South Tyrolean Alpine Association (Alpenverein Südtirol) and the Italian Alpine Club (Club Alpino Italian, CAI), as well as other local groups, periodically organize guided mountain tours.

The region's many mountain shelters are generally open from May or June to October, offering bunk beds and maybe a couple of individual cabins with beds, usually providing snacks, warm meals, and drinks as well. Information on Alpinism may be obtained from the provincial tourism offices and Alpine associations. Local dailies, radio, and television provide detailed meteorological reports and issue avalanche warnings.

WINTER SPORTS   The region is studded with hundreds of prepared ski runs, funiculars, chair lifts, and trails for cross-country skiing. So-called ski passes, permitting the holder to use all winter sports installations and special bus services in a given area at a flat rate during a number of days, can be bought from tourism offices and hotels. Many hotels and pensions offer package deals with reduced rates for rooms and meals during "white weeks" from mid-January to mid-February. Hotel rates are highest during the period from Christmas Eve to January 7.

HUNTING AND FISHING   The hunting season in the region generally lasts from the beginning of September to mid-December. Visiting hunters need special permits and have to pay shooting fees. Short-term licenses for fishing in the many trout streams and lakes of South Tyrol, the Trentino, and the Dolomites may be obtained from the local tourism offices. Information: Provincial Office for Hunting and Fisheries, 6 Brennerstrasse,

39100 Bolzano, telephone 0471–995171, and the tourism agencies of the provinces of Trento and Belluno.

ALPINE EMERGENCIES   South Tyrol and the neighboring provinces of Trento and Belluno are well equipped for coping with mountaineering and skiing accidents. The Italian police forces, Alpine guides, managers of Alpine refuges, and personnel of sports installations include many persons experienced in rescue and first-aid work. Helicopters of the Alpine Rescue Service stand by at all times.

ACCOMMODATIONS   Hotels and pensions in Italy are officially classified in five categories, symbolized by one star (plain) to five stars (luxury). Actually there are hardly any five-star establishments in the region because extra-stiff taxes burden enterprises in this top tier. Almost all of the luxury houses modestly declare themselves to belong to the four-star class but add an "S" (meaning super) to the four stars, as if to say "We are better than that, really." Many full-service houses give preference to guests who in addition to breakfast take also at least one major meal—usually dinner—on the premises. Dinnertime in South Tyrol is early by Italian standards, usually 7:00 or 7:30 P.M., somewhat later in the Dolomites and in the Trentino. Even first-class (four-star) hotels and pensions will often insist that guests be punctual for the main meals. "Hotel garni" is the trade term for an establishment offering rooms and breakfast but no restaurant service. Many hotels and pensions throughout the region are closed in November, some also between the week after Easter until the beginning of June, whereas others are open only from Easter week to November. A large number of establishments in the area have been run by successive generations of the same family.

Plenty of private home owners throughout the area let rooms for a night or longer periods. The traveler is directed to them by listings available from the local tourism office or by the ubiquitous signs "Zimmer" and "Camere" (rooms). Over the last few decades certain unofficial standards for such short-term rental accommodations have evolved in South Tyrol and in the neighboring provinces. The rooms often come with wood paneling and modern-rustic furniture, are always clean, usually have their own bathroom or shower stand, and increasingly have also their own color television set. Breakfast is regularly provided and often ample: coffee, tea, or chocolate; rolls and breads; butter, jam, and honey; eggs on request; and customarily also cold cuts and cheese. Staying in a private home instead of in a hotel, the visitor not only saves money, but may also have a chance to observe Alpine family life.

LANGUAGES   Italian is most useful throughout the region because German-speaking and Ladin-speaking local people are either fluent in it or at least have a good working knowledge of the language. German speakers in South Tyrol will appreciate it if they are addressed in their own language and usually switch readily from their dialect into standard German to make it easier for the stranger to understand them. Relatively few Italian speakers in the area understand or speak any German. As for Ladin and the Ladins, see chapter 7. An increasing number of persons in South Tyrol and the neighboring provinces, especially younger ones, understand English.

BEST TIMES TO VISIT; WEATHER   My own favorite period for a trip to South Tyrol is May, when the sun is already strong and the Alpine flowers on the high plateaus dazzle the hiker. Guests from Belgium, the Netherlands, and Germany flock to the region in June to climb mountains, hike, play tennis, or swim to build up an early tan. High-season rates start in the hotels by mid-July. Italians from Milan to Palermo take over the area in August, especially around the national-religious Ferragosto festival (Assumption), August 15. The days shorten, but the sun is still benevolent and the colors and weather are mellow in September and October. The luminous autumn days attract well-heeled guests from all over Europe to Merano for the horse races and the grape cure, while the towns on the Wine Road celebrate vintage festivals. The first snow, often already in late November, ushers in a brilliant, regionwide winter season with activity on all slopes and après-ski until dawn, culminating during the Christmas holidays and followed by the "white weeks" in January and February. Easter week may afford a last chance for skiing but may also provide a preview of Alpine spring glory. Summer skiing is practiced on the Stelvio Pass (page 103) and on a few other heights.

The valleys and mountains south of the main crest of the Alps receive much more sun all around the year than those north of it and enjoy more stable atmospheric conditions. Yet in South Tyrol and in the Dolomites, too, the weather may be treacherous. Climbers setting out on a fair morning may later find themselves enveloped in fog, drenched by rain on the heights, or in the midst of a snowstorm.

In the valleys, rainstorms sometimes cause rock or mud slides, obstructing highways and occasionally railroad tracks. After a spell of rain in summer, a period of fair weather may be expected when the evenings are cool and fresh snow is visible on the peaks in the morning.

Föhn is a warm southerly wind that may also spring up during cold winters; it is the tailpiece of the sirocco, which periodically dumps uncounted tons of sand from the Sahara on Italy. When the Föhn blows, the air seems to take on a glassy quality, distant mountains appear close and in sharp outline, and forests look almost black from afar. In winter, sudden Föhn greatly increases the danger of avalanches. The glacier that yielded the Iceman (chapter 2) was found at the time covered with a layer of brown North African sand that a recent Föhn had blown as far north as Mount Similaun, contributing to the melting of the glacier ice.

Traverse glaciers only with a local guide. If there are broad crevasses, the guide will insist that at least three persons, roped together securely, undertake to cross the glacier.

FOOD AND DRINK   The northern Italian and Tyrolean cuisines blend in pleasant ways and are enriched by influences from the Friuli region and Venice as well as from Vienna and southern Germany. The prime local specialty is *Speck*, flue-cured ham. Today, alas, almost all the *Speck* you'll get is an industrial product turned out by quick treatment in a smoke chamber. To sample genuine *Bauernspeck* (peasant *Speck*) that for months has hung in the chimney of a farmhouse, one has to have good local connections or must climb to the highest mountain farms. Its characteristic taste is quite different from what you get as *Speck* in plastic wrappers at the supermarket. Industrial *Speck* comes today from anywhere in northern Italy and is marketed throughout the nation.

The typical robust mountaineers' dish is *Knödel*, Italianized as *canederli*. These are large dumplings prepared in at least two dozen versions and eaten in soups, as a side order with pork and other meat, as a principal course together with vegetables or salad, or as a sweet confection for dessert. A Tyrolean classic is *Speckknödel*—dumplings the size of a tennis ball made of small cuts of stale white bread, eggs, onions, chives, and parsley, containing little chunks of *Speck*. *Leberknödel* are liver dumplings served in broth, and *Marillenknödel* is the name for golf ball–size potato-dough dumplings, each containing a pitted apricot. Cornmeal, grated cheese, and other ingredients too are used for *Knödel*. The dumplings should be neither too solid nor too soft. Purists insist that *Knödel* must never be cut with a knife but have to be eaten with a fork; however, I have been served large *Knödel* in Tyrolean eating places that came in thick slices, precut with a knife the way one often gets them in Czech restaurants as *knedliky*.

Pasta dishes are by now everyday fare in South Tyrol, although Italians will complain that they are often overcooked instead of al dente. A Tyrolean form of pasta frequently found on local restaurant menus is *Schlutzkrapfen*—spinach-filled ravioli served with plenty of melted butter.

Among soups, one made with plump pearl barley and known as *Gerstsuppe* is specifically Tyrolean; old people in the region tell me they ate barley soup almost every day in the year when they were children. Vegetable soups too are popular in South Tyrol, but for a rich minestrone you'd better go to one of the more southerly provinces of Italy.

The provinces of Bolzano, Belluno, and Trento are united in their partiality for polenta, sharing their taste for the cornmeal mush with the rest of the Friuli region, with Venice, with the Bergamo hills, and with the Swiss Ticino. Italians from other parts of the nation in fact call those northerners *polentoni* (polenta eaters), an ethnic-culinary label suggesting stolidity.

To people so characterized, instead, the word *polenta* conjures up a vision of frugal life in the mountains; some poor families in the not-too-distant past used to eat polenta for breakfast, lunch, and dinner the year around, seeing meat on their tables only on the most important feast days, and as a result suffered from scurvy because of the lack of vitamins. To obtain the chewy texture of genuine polenta, the cornmeal must be allowed to trickle into a pot of salty, boiling water and be stirred slowly with a wooden ladle for at least an hour. Today few restaurant chefs have the patience or manpower to go through this simple but lengthy procedure, and guests therefore get a bland pap that doesn't deserve the name *polenta*. Generally polenta is a side order with meat, codfish, or other dishes; but it may also be cut into slices, roasted, and combined with, for instance, gorgonzola cheese as an entrée.

Goulash, often served with polenta, is made in the region according to Hungarian-Viennese recipes, with large cubes of beef, pork fat, onions, and maybe a dash of red wine. *Gröstl* ("roasteds"), another typically Tyrolean dish, is a seasoned mix-ture of sliced potatoes and small pieces of veal or beef, roasted in olive oil or butter. During the hunting season many eating places feature roast saddle of deer and other game.

As for fish, trout is offered throughout the area, coming boiled ("blue"), roasted, or steamed in aluminum foil. It's a rare delight when the trout has been caught in a stream a few hours earlier, but most of the fish in restaurants come from hatcheries.

The region is rich in edible mushrooms, although they don't grow in the same quantity every year. Indigenous to the Alpine forests are the brown-capped porcini (in German: *Steinpilze* or *Herrenpilze*) of the genus *Boletus edulis* and egg-yellow chanterelles, locally called *Pfifferlinge*.

In the field of desserts South Tyrol is a province of the confectioners' empire of Vienna, with apple strudels, poppyseed strudels, sweet-curd (*Topfen*) strudels, *Krapfen* (sweet buns), and lush tortes. Such high-calorie bombes are also served in many

Vienna-style coffeehouses together with whipped-cream-topped cappuccino. Italy has contributed gelato and, lately, tiramisù (made with powdered cocoa, sugar, and soft, sweet cheese) to the Alpine dessert list.

Bread is baked mostly with rye flour and turned out in shapes that may vary from valley to valley. During holiday seasons and for other festive occasions, bakeries produce special breads containing raisins, almonds, and other goodies, as well as gingerbread. The blond, Vienna-type *Semmel* (rolls), baked with wheat flour, that most hotels and pensions offer for breakfast have a bland taste and are often spongy.

Pizza has become ubiquitous throughout the region during the last few decades, and pizzerias may also be found in small villages. Quite a few South Tyrolean entrepreneurs have imported pizza cooks from southern Italy.

≈ The sunny slopes framing the Adige/Etsch River and its tributaries have for many centuries been covered with vineyards. Most of the wine produced in South Tyrol and the Trentino is red, and the local wineries and vintners' cooperatives have succeeded in greatly improving its quality during the last few decades, winning new markets in the rest of Italy and in northern Europe. Bottles with the notation *Denominazione d'origine controllata*, or DOC (Name of origin guaranteed), are to be preferred. Cheaper wines that come in bottles closed with metal caps or in open carafes are uneven.

The best-known South Tyrolean wine is Kalterersee, often labeled in Italian as Lago di Caldaro; it is grown—or pretends to have been grown—around Kaltern/Caldaro (page 134), the main town on the Wine Road. It is a claret-type product based on the vernatsch grape and should be drunk no later than a couple of years after harvesting. Other reds that improve through aging, especially pinot noir and merlot varieties, are also grown in some vineyards in South Tyrol and especially in the Trentino. Merlot and valpolicella from the Venetian mainland are widely drunk in the Dolomites.

The production of dry white wines of the pinot blanc and chardonnay kinds has increased in the region during the last several years. The village of Tramin on the Wine Road has lent its name to gewürztraminer, a rather heavy white wine with a spicy bouquet that connoisseurs usually associate with the French Alsace region, where it is made in quantity; it was originally grown near Tramin, and a few vineyards in the area and around Brixen/Bressanone still yield that variety of whites.

South Tyrol's own brewery is in the Forst suburb of Merano; it claims to use water from the resort's curative springs. Forst beers are drunk all over the region. In the Dolomites and in the Trentino, beers from Trieste and Friuli are also widely available, while more expensive brews are imported from the Czech Republic, Denmark, Germany, and the Netherlands.

Grappa, a colorless brandy distilled from the residues of grapes in wine making, is the classic aperitif, after-dinner drink, and all-round pick-me-up in the region. It is a macho beverage fancied by mountaineers, hunters, and other outdoors people and is offered in great variety from rough to comparatively smooth. Local distilleries also produce brandies based on apples, pears, apricots, cherries, and other fruits or on Alpine herbs; some are deceptively suave but pack a remarkable punch.

SHOPPING; BUSINESS HOURS   Things to buy in South Tyrol, the Dolomites, and the Trentino include Italian fashions, shoes and other leatherware, wines, *speck*, fruits, and wood carvings. In addition to the Italian nationwide department store and supermarket chains, like Rinascente and Standa, the regional supermarket organization Despar has stores in many towns.

Shopping hours are generally from 8:00 or 8:30 A.M. to noon and from 3 to 6 or 7 P.M. Monday to Friday; 8:30 A.M. to noon Saturday. During the main tourist seasons some stores are also open Saturday afternoon and Sunday morning. Banks are generally open from 8 A.M. to 1 P.M. and from 3 to 4 P.M. Monday to Friday, and a growing number of them have automatic teller machines accessible around the clock. Foreign money and traveler's checks can be exchanged at the official rate at the local tourism offices, which usually keep longer hours than the banks. Post office hours are from 8:00 A.M. to 1:30 P.M. Monday to Friday, with afternoon and Saturday morning service in major towns.

After paying in a restaurant, cafe, tavern, espresso bar, hotel, or store in Italy, you ought to be given a formal receipt (*ricevuta fiscale*) and should keep it at least for some time, because uniformed or plainclothes officers of the Guardia di Finanza (fiscal police) are carrying out spot checks to make sure the Italian Treasury gets value-added tax (the Italian abbreviation is IVA), a kind of sales tax. If you cannot produce such a receipt after a purchase of goods or services, you are liable to be fined together with the seller.

INFORMATION   South Tyrol Tourism Office, 11-12 Piazza Parrocchia/Pfarrplatz, I-39100 Bolzano/Bozen, phone (39–471) 993808, fax 975448; Tourism Service of the Autonomous Province of Trento, phone (39–461) 896555; Tourism Office of Belluno, phone (39–473) 908149. Also note the telephone and fax numbers of the tourism offices in the major centers of the region in the Appendix.

APPENDIX

Accommodation and Food on the
Sunny Side of the Alps

Places in the autonomous province of Bolzano/Südtirol are listed below alphabetically according to their official Italian names, followed by their traditional Tyrolean-German or Ladin names. The listings also include a few centers in the Italian province of Belluno, in the Swiss canton of Graubünden/Grisons, and in the Austrian regions of East Tyrol and Carinthia.

"ZIP" in the following listings stands for what in Italian usage is known as CAP (Codice di Avviamento Postale) and for the Swiss and Austrian mail delivery area codes. "TAC" means telephone area code. It is preceded in Italy, Switzerland, and Austria by a zero, which has to be omitted if a call is made from some other country. For instance, if the number 12345 in Italy is to be reached from the United States and its area code is 0471, dial or press 011-39-471-12345. The country code for Italy is 39, for Switzerland 41, and for Austria 43. "I" stands for tourist information office and is followed by its telephone number and, if it exists, its fax number.

The hotels and restaurants listed are marked with a (T) for top-rated, (M) for medium range, or (P) for plain. Quality, decor, service, and price were considered in these appraisals.

The listings comprise only establishments that I have investigated personally or that have been concurrently nominated by two or more reliable informants. Many more hotels and restaurants would qualify; their omission means only that I have been unable to recommend them on the basis of personal experience or of research by knowledgeable friends. Only major centers and some key places were considered. Travelers and visitors will almost invariably find some suitable hotel, inn, or private home for spending the night and won't have any trouble getting a meal, snack, or drink even in small villages and hamlets.

BARBIANO/BARBIAN   ZIP 39040; TAC 0471; I phone 654411.

HOTEL AND RESTAURANT:

Messner Hof (P), Tre Chiese/Drei Kirchen, phone 650059.

BOLZANO/BOZEN   ZIP 39100; TAC 0471; I phone 970660, fax 980300.

HOTELS:

Park Hotel Laurin (T), 4 Via Laurin/Laurinstrasse, phone 980500, fax 970953.

Luna/Mondschein (M), Via Piave, phone 975642, fax 975577.

Città di Bolzano/Stadthotel (M), 21 Piazza Walther/Waltherplatz, phone 975221, fax 976688.

Croce Bianca/Weisses Kreuz (P), 3 Piazza del Grano/Kornplatz, phone 977552.

RESTAURANTS:

Amadè (T), 8 Vicolo Cà de' Bezzi/Batzenhäusl-Gasse, phone 971278.

Belle Époque (T), 4 Via Laurin/Laurinstrasse, phone 980500.

Batzenhäusl (M), 30 Via Andrea Hofer/Andreas Hofer Strasse, phone 976183.

Pizzeria Partenope (P), 13 Via Marconi/Marconi Strasse, phone 97017.

BRAIES/PRAGS   ZIP 39039; TAC 0474; I phone 78660, fax same number.

HOTEL AND RESTAURANT:

  Lago di Braies/Pragser Wildsee (M), 27 San Vito/St. Veit, phone 78602, fax 78752.

BRENNERO/BRENNER   ZIP 39041; TAC 0472; I phone 62372, fax 62580.

HOTEL AND RESTAURANT:

  Posta/Post (P), 29 Via San Valentino/St. Valentin-Strasse, phone 61120.

BRESSANONE/BRIXEN   ZIP 39042; TAC 0472; I phone 836401, fax 836067.

HOTELS:

  Elefant (T), 4 Via Rio Bianco/Weisslahn-Strasse, phone 832750, fax 836579.

  Dominik (T), 13 Via Terzo di Sotto/Unterdrittel-Gasse, phone 830144.

  Jarolim (M), 1 Piazza della Stazione/Bahnhofplatz, phone 836230, fax 833155.

  Al Sole/Sonne (M), 8 Via Sant'Erardo/Erhardgasse, phone 832191, fax 837347.

HEALTH FARM:

  Casa di Cura/Kurhaus Dr. von Guggenberg (T), 17 Via Terzo di Sotto/Unterdrittel-Gasse, phone 835525, fax 834014.

RESTAURANTS:

  Elefant (T), 4 Via Rio Bianco/Weisslahn-Strasse, phone 832750.

  Fink (M), 4 Via Portici Minori/Kleine Lauben, phone 834883.

  Oste Scuro/Finsterwirt (M), 3 Vicolo del Duomo/Domgasse, phone 832344.

WINE TAVERN:

  Stiftskeller Neustift (P), Novacella/Neustift, phone 836189.

BRUNICO/BRUNECK   ZIP 39031; TAC 0474; I phone 555722, fax 555544.

APPENDIX

HOTELS:

Royal Hotel Hinterhuber (T), in the hamlet of Riscone/Reischach, nearly 2 miles (3 kilometers) southeast of the town, phone 21221, fax 20848.

Andreas Hofer (M), Via Campo Tures/Tauferer-Strasse, phone 85469, fax 85813.

Posta/Post (M), 9 Via Bastioni/Graben, phone 555127, fax 31603.

Bologna (P), 1 Via Leonardo da Vinci, phone 555917, fax 555288.

RESTAURANT:

Blauer Bock (M), phone 85834; in the hamlet of Teodone/Dietenheim, less than 1 mile (1.3 kilometers) northeast of the town.

CALDARO/KALTERN   ZIP 39052; TAC 0471; I phone 963169, fax 963469.

HOTELS:

Kartheiner Hof (T), 22 Weinstrasse, phone 963240, fax 963145.

Europa (M), 21 Via Europa/Europa-Strasse, phone 963370.

RESTAURANT:

Seegarten (M), 17 St. Josef am See, phone 963260; on the lake, with guest rooms.

CAMPO TURES/SAND IN TAUFERS   ZIP 39032; TAC 0474; I phone 678076, fax 678922.

HOTELS:

Feldmüllerhof (M), 9 Via del Castello/Schlossweg, St. Moritzen, phone 678127, fax 68935.

Schloss Schrottwinkel (M), 15 Ahrntaler-Strasse, phone 678100; an old castle.

RESTAURANTS:

Alte Mühle (M), St. Moritzen, phone 678077; with guest rooms.

Flankensteiner (M), 19 Ahrntaler-Strasse, phone 678029; with guest rooms.

CASTELROTTO/KASTELRUTH   ZIP 39040; TAC 0471; I phone 706333, fax 705188.

HOTELS:

Cavallino d'Oro/Goldenes Rössl (M), 2 Via Buehl/Buehlweg, phone 706337, fax 707172.

Madonna (M), 35 Kleinmühlweg, phone 706194, fax 705363.

Toni (P), 5 0.-von-Wolkenstein-Strasse, phone 706306.

RESTAURANT:

Posthotel Lamm (M), 3 Krausenplatz, phone 706343, fax 707063; with guest rooms.

CHIUSA/KLAUSEN   ZIP 39043; TAC 0472; I phone 47424, fax 47244.

HOTEL:

Post (M), 41 Tinneplatz, phone 47514.

RESTAURANT:

Grauer Bär (M), 3 Unterstadt, phone 47544; with guest rooms.

COLLE ISARCO/GOSSENSASS   ZIP 39040; TAC 0472; I phone 62372, fax 62580.

HOTELS:

Juliane (M), 32 Colle Isarco/Gossensass, phone 62450, fax 62092.

Gudrun (M), 21 Colle Isarco/Gossensass, phone 62318, fax 62106.

CORTINA D'AMPEZZO   ZIP 32043; TAC 0436; I phone 3231, fax 3235.

HOTELS:

Miramonti Majestic (T), 103 Pezziè, phone 4201, fax 867019; 1.5 miles (about 2 kilometers) south of the town, with a nine-hole golf course.

De la Poste (T), 14 Piazza Roma, phone 4271, fax 868435.

Menardi (M), 110 Via Maion, phone 2400, fax 862163.

Villa Nevada (P), 64 Via Ronco, phone 4778.

RESTAURANTS:

Il Meloncino (T), 17 Gillardon, phone 861043; nearly 3 miles (5 kilometers) west of the town.

El Toulà (T), 123 Via Ronco, phone 3339.
De la Poste (M), 14 Piazza Roma, phone 4271.

CORVARA IN BADIA/KURFAR   ZIP 39033; TAC 0471; I phone
836176, fax 836540.

HOTELS:

Cappella (T), 100 Colfosco/Kolfuschg, phone 836183, fax 836561.
La Perla (T), 44 Via Pedecovara, phone 836132, fax 836568.
Col Alto (M), 47 Pescosta, phone 836129, fax 836066.
La Fontana (P), 65 Via di Centro/Zentrum, phone 836000, fax 836707.

RESTAURANTS:

La Perla (T), 44 Via Pedecovara, phone 836132.
La Tambra Selfservice (P), 159 Via Pescosta, phone 836281.

DOBBIACO/TOBLACH   ZIP 39034; TAC 0474; I phone 72132,
fax 72730.

HOTELS:

Santer (T), 4 Via Alemagna, phone 72142, fax 72797.
Cristallo-Walch (M), 11 Viale Roma, phone 72138, fax 72755.
Urthaler (P), 5 Via Castello/Herbstenburg-Strasse, phone 72241, fax 973050.

RESTAURANT:

Gratschwirt (M), 1 Grazze/Gratsch, phone 72293, fax 72915; about 1 mile (1.5 kilometers) east of the town; with guest rooms.

FIÈ ALLO SCILIAR/VÖLS AM SCHLERN   ZIP 39050; TAC
0471; I phone 725047, fax 725488.

HOTELS:

Emmy (T), 5 Putzesweg, Obervöls, phone 725006, fax 725484.
Völser Heubad (M), 12 Obervöls, phone 725020; with hay baths.

RESTAURANT:

Tschafon (M), 1 Bozner-Strasse, phone 725024; reservation required.

GLORENZA/GLURNS ZIP 39020; TAC 0473; I phone 81097.
HOTEL:
Krone (P), 9 Stadtplatz, phone 81440.
RESTAURANT:
Posta/Zur Post (M), 15 Florastrasse, phone 81208.

HEILIGENBLUT, AUSTRIA ZIP 9844; TAC 04824; I phone 2002.
HOTEL AND RESTAURANT:
Senger (M), phone 2215, fax 22159.

KLAGENFURT, AUSTRIA ZIP 9020; TAC 0463; I phone 537223.
HOTELS:
Musil (T), 14 10.-Oktober-Strasse, phone 511660, fax 516765, with a good cafe.
Moser-Verdino (M), 2 Domgasse, phone 57878, fax 516765.
Zlami (P), 16 Getreidegasse, phone 55416.
RESTAURANTS:
A la Carte (T), 2 Khevenhüller-Strasse, phone 516651.
Zum Augustin (M), 2 Pfarrhofgasse, phone 513992.

LAION/LAJEN ZIP 39040; TAC 0471; I phone 655633.
HOTEL:
Ansitz Fonteklaus (M), 4 Freins, phone 655654; a reconverted old mansion.
RESTAURANT:
Sonne (P), 32 Dorf, phone 655659; with guest rooms.

LIENZ, AUSTRIA ZIP 9900; TAC 04852; I phone 4747.
HOTEL AND RESTAURANT:
Traube (M), 14 Hauptplatz, phone 6444, fax 64184.

MARIA TRENS ZIP 39040; TAC 0472; I phone 67390.
HOTEL AND RESTAURANT:
Bircher (M), 70 Maria Trens, phone 67122.

MERANO/MERAN   ZIP 39012; TAC 0473; I phone 235223, fax 235524.

HOTELS:

Palace (T), 2 Via Cavour, phone 34734.

Kurhotel Schloss Rundegg (T), 2 Via Scena/Schennastrasse, phone 33464, fax 37200; a health and beauty farm in a sixteenth-century castle.

Mendelhof/Mendola (M), 45 Winkelweg, phone 236130, fax 236481.

Mondschein (P), 47 Pfarrgasse, phone 32176.

RESTAURANTS:

Andrea (T), 44 Via Galilei, phone 37400.

Villa Mozart (T), 26 Via Markus, phone 30630, fax 211355; also a hotel. Reservations indispensable.

Forsterbräu (M), 90 Via della Libertà/Freiheitsstrasse, phone 36535; a brewery-owned brasserie.

Terlaner Weinstube (M), 231 Portici/Lauben.

Seibstock's Bistro (P), 204 Portici/Lauben, phone 32605.

MÜSTAIR,   CANTON   GRAUBÜNDEN/GRISONS, SWITZERLAND   ZIP 7537; TAC 082; I phone 85000, fax 85760.

HOTEL:

Helvetia (P), phone 85555, fax 85760.

NATURNO/NATURNS   ZIP 39025; TAC 0473; I phone 87287, fax 88270.

HOTELS:

Feldhof (M), 4 Rathausstrasse, phone 87264.

Sonnenhof (M), 2 Rathausstrasse, phone 870250, fax 666050.

Schmiedhof (P), 3 Schlossweg/Via Castello, phone 87428.

RESTAURANTS:

Schnalserhof (M), 121 Via Val Venosta/Vinschgauer Strasse, phone 87219, fax 88253; about 1.5 miles (2 kilometers) west of the town, with guest rooms.

Zum Adler (P), Hauptplatz, phone 87252.

APPENDIX

ORTISEI/URTIJËI/ST. ULRICH   ZIP 39046; TAC 0471; I phone 796328, fax 796749.

HOTELS:

Adler (T), Via Rezia, phone 796203, fax 796210.

Posta-Cavallino Bianco (M), 22 Via Rezia, phone 796392, fax 796517.

Rainell (M), 19 Vidalong Strasse, Oltratorrente/Unterwasser, phone 796145, fax 796279.

Arnaria (M), 15 Via Arnaria, Roncadizza/Runggaditsch, phone 796649, fax 798516.

Cherubini (P), 36 Via J. B. Purger, phone 796194.

RESTAURANTS:

Cucina Veneta (M), 162 Via Rezia, phone 796568.

Pizzeria Tennis (P), 5 Via Arnaria, phone 798018.

RENON/RITTEN   ZIP 39054; TAC 0471; I phone 356100, fax 356799.

HOTELS:

Parkhotel Holzner (M), 18 Dorf, Oberbozen/Soprabolzano, phone 345231, fax 345593.

Bemelmans Post (M), 8 Dorfstrasse, Collalbo/Klobenstein, phone 356127, fax 356531.

Maier (M), 2 Wolfsgruben/Costalovara, phone 345114, fax 345615.

Linde (P), 31 Michael-Gamper-Weg, Collalbo/Klobenstein, phone 356317.

RESTAURANT:

Weber im Moos (M), 3 Anna di Sotto/Unterinn, phone 356707; with guest rooms.

SAN CANDIDO/INNICHEN   ZIP 39038; TAC 0474; I phone 73149, fax 73677.

HOTELS:

Cavallino Bianco/Weisses Rössl (M), 1 Via Duca Tassilo, phone 73135, fax 73733; with good restaurant.

Schmieder (M), 16 Via Duca Tassilo, phone 73144.

225

ST. MARIA IM MÜNSTERTAL, CANTON GRAUBÜNDEN/ GRISONS, SWITZERLAND   ZIP 7536; TAC 082; I phone 85727.

HOTEL:

Schweizerhof (M), phone 85124, fax 85009.

SANTA CRISTINA VALGARDENA/ST. CHRISTINA IN GRÖDEN   ZIP 39047; TAC 0471; I phone 793046, fax 793198.

HOTELS:

Sporthotel Monte Pana (T), 45 Monte Pana, phone 793600, fax 793527; at 5,371 feet (1,637 meters) altitude, 2 miles (3 kilometers) south of the village.

Dosses (M), 115 Via Dursan, phone 793326, fax 793711.

RESTAURANT:

Posta (M), 32 Via Dursan, phone 792078.

SAN VIGILIO DI MAREBBE/AL PLAN DE MAREO/ ST. VIGIL IN ENNEBURG   ZIP 39030; TAC 0471; I phone 50137, fax 501566.

HOTEL:

Almhof Hotel Call (M), 43 Villaggio/Dorf, phone 501043, fax 501569; with restaurant.

SELVA DI VALGARDENA/SËLVA/WOLKENSTEIN

ZIP 39048; TAC 0471; I phone 795122, fax 794245.

HOTELS:

Sporthotel Gran Baita (M), 145 Via Maisules, phone 795210, fax 795080; with restaurant.

Tyrol (M), Via Puez, phone 795270; with restaurant.

SESTO/SEXTEN   ZIP 39030; TAC 0474; I phone 70310, fax 70318.

HOTELS:

Rainer (M), 40 St. Josefs-Strasse, Moos, phone 70366.

Sextnerhof (M), 13 Dolomiten-Strasse, phone 70314, fax 70161.

Alpenhof (P), 1 Panoramaweg, Phone 70317.

APPENDIX

RESTAURANT:
  Monika (M), 2 Parkweg, phone 70384.

SIUSI/SEIS AM SCHLERN   ZIP 39040; TAC 0471; I phone 706124, fax 707134.

HOTEL AND RESTAURANT:
  Schwarzer Adler-Unterwirt (M), 7 Via Laurino, phone 706146.

TIROLO/DORF TIROL   ZIP 39019; TAC 0473; I phone 93314, fax 93012.

HOTELS:
  Erika (M), 39 Haupt-Strasse, phone 93338, fax 93066.
  Sole/Sonne (P), 4 Schlossweg, phone 93329.

RESTAURANT:
  Gartner (M), 65 Haupt-Strasse, phone 93414.

VILLACH, AUSTRIA   ZIP 9500; TAC 04242; I phone 24444.

HOTEL:
  Post (M), 26 Hauptplatz, phone 26101, fax 26101–420.

RESTAURANT:
  Trattoria Adriatico (M), 5 Bambergergasse, phone 26374.

VIPITENO/STERZING   ZIP 39049; TAC 0472; I phone 765325, fax 765441.

HOTELS:
  Aquila Nera/Schwarzer Adler (M), 1 Stadtplatz, phone 764064, fax 766522.
  Parkhotel Stoetter (M), Bahnhof-Strasse/Via Stazione, phone 765202, fax 766878.
  Post (P), 14 Neustadt, phone 765172.

RESTAURANT:
  Mühlsteiger (M), 1 Stadtplatz, phone 764064.

INDEX

INDEX

INDEX

INDEX

239